Visions Beyond the Veil

H.A. Baker

GodSounds

"Where Faith is Heard"

For more information on our voiceover services
and to see our online store of Christian audio-books
go to **GodSounds.com**

OTHER BOOKS AVAILABLE BY GODSOUNDS, INC.

Like Precious Faith
by Smith Wigglesworth

Divine Healing: A Gift from God
by John G Lake

Intimacy with Jesus: Verse by Verse from the Song of Songs
by Madame Guyon

A Plain Account of Christian Perfection
by John Wesley

Finney Gold: Words that Helped Birth Revival
by Charles Finney

Closer to God
by Meister Eckhart

The Letters of Ignatius
by Ignatius

The printing of this book is dedicated to Rolland & Heidi Baker, as I believe that H.A. Baker is proud of them and rooting them on - *even now*.

CONTENTS

Jesus is Lord.

Introduction

THE CHILDREN AND YOUNG PEOPLE upon whom came this outpouring of the Holy Spirit and through whom came these visions and revelations were members of the Adullam Rescue Mission in Yunnanfu, Yunnan Province, China. For the most part, these children had been beggars in the streets of the city. In some cases they were poor children with one or both parents dead and had been brought to the Home. There were also some prodigals who had run away from their homes in more distant parts of this or adjoining provinces.

But from whatever source they came, these children, mostly boys ranging in ages from six to eighteen, had come to us without previous training in morals and without education. Begging is a sort of "gang" system in which stealing is a profitable part. The morals are what would be expected of a "gang" in a godless land.

The Bible is carefully and daily taught in the Adullam Home, and the gospel is constantly preached. Since the children coming into the home have always been open to the teachings given, before the outpouring of the Holy Spirit recorded below, some of them were doubtless converted, while many had a very good knowledge of the main themes of the Bible.

All who received the Holy Spirit knew enough to believe in one God and to trust in the blood of Christ for salvation. They also prayed for the fullness of the Holy Spirit. They sought Christ. We did not see any one seeking visions or any of the manifestations that were received day by day as all single heartedly prayed and praised the Lord Jesus. He alone was sought and magnified throughout all the weeks of the Spirit's outpouring. In this visitation from the Lord all were treated impartially. The oldest and the youngest, the first arrivals and the latest comers, the best and the worst, all sitting together around their common Father's table were alike treated to His heavenly bounties.

This giving of the Promised Spirit was clearly a love gift of grace "apart from works" or personal merit. It was not something that was worked up. It was something that came down. It was not the result of character building by man from below. It was a blessing of God that came from above.

The Experiences Herein Related are Unexplainable on Natural Ground

The experiences of these Adullam children that are herein related cannot be explained on natural ground, because:

1. These wonders **could not possibly have been the product of the natural minds of these children.** Such uneducated, mentally untrained, unimaginative boys as these could not themselves have conceived of such things.

2. These spiritual experiences, visions, and revelations **could not have been the working of the subconscious mind.** Many of these children were too young, too ignorant, or too recently rescued from heathenism to know the Bible teaching on these subjects.

3. Then, again, these things **cannot be explained by the**

psychology of mental suggestion from others. We ourselves had never seen such visions, never been in meetings where there were such, or read or heard of such visions as were given these children. These experiences were new to all of us.

4. Furthermore, the children **did not get these things from one another.** When the power of the Lord fell in our midst many children were filled with the Spirit at the same time. Those who were in different rooms sometimes had simultaneous visions of the same things. There was no possibility of comparing one with another.

5. **The complete harmony** of these visions covering numberless details is beyond any natural explanation. Even the most ignorant children, who could easily be confused on cross questioning, whether questioned singly or in groups, gave as clear and uniform answers to questions covering great numbers of details as could possibly have been given by eye witnesses of anything.

6. Neither can these experiences be explained as any sort of mental excitement, religious frenzy, natural emotion, nervous state, nor any sort of self-produced condition. This outpouring of the Holy Spirit came upon normal children in a normal state of mind free from all the conditions just mentioned.

The Visions and Revelations Given Adullam are Consistent Supernatural Experiences in the True Church

Supernatural visions and revelations are foundation rocks upon which the Church was established and upon which it stands. The whole Bible, Old and New Testament, is a **supernatural** revelation from God.

In the Old Testament, God revealed his will to men by speaking through prophets by direct inspiration in which the mind of the prophet had no part. The Lord appeared to men and spoke to them in a "voice" with "words." He thus spoke to

Moses, as man speaks to man face to face.1 In the Old Testament, God revealed himself to men in dreams, in visions, and in various kinds of supernatural revelations. Angels brought messages to men and were continually active as God's ambassadors in carrying out His plan of redemption on earth.

The New Testament, likewise, claims to be a **superhuman** revelation. Paul said of the gospel he preached: "Neither did I receive it from man, nor was I taught it, but it came to me through **revelation** of Jesus Christ" (Gal. 1:12). What he wrote in all his epistles was simply a part of this supernatural "revelation of Jesus Christ."

Without such working of the Holy Spirit and without such visions and revelations as were given Adullam there would be no Christianity at all. The true Church, begun in this manner, exists to the present day because just such supernatural manifestations formed the cradle in which it was born and nursed into vigorous life. When Herod would destroy the baby Jesus, the wise men were "warned of God in a dream."2 An angel appeared to Joseph in a dream. One like a man of Macedonia appeared to Paul in a vision. At Corinth the Lord spoke to him "in the night by a vision." When he was praying in the temple at Jerusalem he fell into "a trance" and saw Jesus, who spoke to him, giving him directions for his work. Peter also fell into "a trance" while praying on the house top. He saw a vision and heard the Lord speaking to him in a voice with words. An angel appeared to Cornelius in an open **vision** by day. The whole book of Revelation was given to John as a **supernatural revelation** when he was "in the Spirit." It is a revelation from the Lord who spoke to him in "a great voice," and it is also a record of visions given in the Spirit and through the ministry of angels. Paul either died and went to heaven "out of the body" or was in vision caught up to heaven like our Adullam children and there saw Paradise. He had such an abundance of these supernatural revelations that the Lord had to send him a thorn in the flesh to keep him humble.

Angels, also, had a large part in the work of the first church.

The early disciples were often **protected** and **directed** in their work by **the angels**. In this way they were delivered from imminent danger from earthly powers. An angel spoke to Philip, directing him to Gaza. An angel stood by Paul and talked with him, encouraging and directing him. Cornelius, his household, and his friends were led unto the way of salvation and into the baptism of the Holy Spirit through the words of an angel who came to him. This angel, appearing in bright apparel, talked with him, directing him to send for Peter and then departed. When Peter was in prison an angel rescued him. This angel loosened the chains from Peter's hands, told him to put on his garments and shoes, opened the prison door and the city gate that was locked, and led Peter into the street.

Greatest of all the supernatural manifestations in the early church were those of the mighty Holy Spirit, who came to that Church just as the Lord had promised He would come after Christ ascended to the Father.

That first church did not **read** prayers. Neither did that first church **say** prayers. That first church prayed to God from the heart, and God directly and **supernaturally** answered these heart cries. When the disciples were in danger they got together and prayed to God. This was not **formal** praying; it was not a cringing, heartless, carefully worded prayer meeting for men's ears. Everybody prayed at the same time; everybody cried to God in a **loud voice**. This was a special prayer meeting for one great need.

When God answered, everybody knew He answered. The Holy Spirit shook the house in which these people were praying, and every one was "filled with the Holy Spirit," with a mighty superhuman power. They then went out spreading gospel fire in the very face of death.

The early church had a **living** God. Through the Holy Spirit they had Christ in their midst. He worked in them and through them supernaturally by gifts of the Holy Spirit: "For to one is given through the Spirit the word of wisdom; and to another the word of knowledge; to another faith...; to another workings of miracles…; to another gifts of healings…; to another prophecy…; to another discerning of spirits…; to another kinds of tongues…; and to another interpretation of tongues" (I Cor. 12:7-10) .

Where is the Living God who brought our fathers up out of Egypt with a mighty hand before the eyes of the heathen? Where is our God who once answered in a voice that men could **hear**, yea, whose voice shook the whole earth? What has become of the God who from the time the earth was created sent his angels to walk and to talk with his people?

What has become of the angels?

And the Christ of the Bible? Where is He? Have they taken away our Lord, so we cannot find where they have laid Him?

What has become of His "Promise"? Christ said that if He should go away it would be better than ever for His people, for God would walk with them more than in all the ages past. His Promise was, "It is expedient for you that I go away, for if I do not go away the Comforter will not come unto you; but if I go, I will send Him unto you." "He that believeth on me, the works that I do shall he do also."3

Our Lord has gone. Where, oh, where is the Holy Spirit that was to come to take His place; to carry on His uncompleted task; to work in the midst of His Church in signs and wonders and gifts of the Holy Spirit? Has God died? If so, when? Or has God withdrawn so far away that He cannot hear? Can not God talk any more? Have the angels deserted us for some other universe? If so, when did they forsake us? After all, is the Holy Spirit, this great power of God, this great substitute for the miracle working Christ, the Christ whose words the winds and waves obeyed, whose words burst the tombs, is this Great Substitute just a gentle influence? Where is the Holy Spirit Who shook and filled a whole house of praying disciples and through them shook a world?

If ever there was a Living God, if ever there were angels, if ever there was a wonder working Christ, if the Holy Spirit was ever given, if the Bible is a supernatural revelation from God, then such trances, visions, revelations, and workings of the Holy Spirit as have been given Adullam are supernatural visitations from God such as we should expect.

These trances, visions, revelations, and supernatural manifestations are normal experiences in the supernaturally founded, supernaturally filled, and supernaturally directed Church of the New Testament, the only Church the Bible tells or foretells anything about.

CHAPTER 1

MIGHTY OUTPOURING OF THE HOLY SPIRIT

MORNING PRAYER MEETING WAS lasting longer than usual. The older children left the room one by one to begin their studies in the school-room, while a few of the smaller boys remained on their knees, praying earnestly. The Lord was near; we all felt the presence of the Holy Spirit in our midst. Some who had gone out returned to the room.

Such a mighty conviction of sin—a thing for which we had prayed so long—came to all, that with tears streaming from their eyes and arms uplifted they cried unto the Lord for forgiveness for their sins, which now seemed so black. One after another went down under the mighty power of the Holy Spirit until more than twenty were prostrate on the floor. When I saw that the Lord was doing a most unusual thing in our midst, I slipped over to the school room and told the boys that if they felt led to come and pray they might be excused from their school work. In a short time the Chinese teacher was left sitting alone by the table. All his pupils having returned to the prayer room, they were whole-heartedly praying and praising the Lord. When the teacher realized there was nothing for him to do, he started for his home. I had not invited him in with the children, for, although he has been with us a long time, he seemed utterly dead, rather, not yet alive to any spiritual conception of the gospel. Having gone but a short distance from the house, he returned. When he entered the prayer room nobody noticed him, for every one was intent on his own business with the Lord. The teacher went to the farthest corner of the room, where, for the first time in his life, he knelt down and tried to pray.

As the Lord's power was so very manifest, I felt it best to leave the young man by himself and not to intrude on what I knew must be the work of the Spirit and of the Spirit alone. It was not long before I noticed the teacher with arms uplifted, tears on his face, pleading with the Lord to forgive his sins, which I heard him say were so very, very many. He being proud, for him to humble himself thus in the presence of his pupils meant a real Holy Spirit conviction of sin.

The meeting went on hour after hour, the children showing no desire to leave. I had nothing to do or say; the Lord seemed to have complete control; I just tried to keep out of His way.

As the children in visions saw the awfulness of hell, the anguish of lost souls, and the indescribable hellish power of the devil and his angels their agonized crying was beyond anything I had ever heard or imagined. It was all real to them. Many saw themselves bound and dragged to the very brink of hell, which to them was no myth but an awful reality. Condemnation for sins and the power of the devil over them was terrorizing in its reality. But freedom from this evil power through the grace of the Lord Jesus was just as real. When they experienced this loosening power from the clutch of the evil one their salvation was as real as had been their condemnation. Their joy, laughter, and peace of soul in the knowledge of what they had been saved from gave them an experience from which I am sure they will never be able to depart.

Since from early morning they had all been in the very presence of the Lord, by the time their late afternoon meal was ready I thought surely the service for the day was over. Not so. Some left the prayer room for a short time, but all were soon back, saying they wanted to wait upon the Lord all night. This was something decidedly new to us, for previously an hour service was too long for some of them. We had long wanted them to pray more; now that they were willing, why refuse them? Not a child went to sleep until a late hour that night; not until six o'clock the next morning were the last voices stilled in the prayer and praise service that had lasted over twenty hours with scarcely a pause. -Josephine Baker.

Continuous Weeks of the Latter Rain

After the first two days of the mighty outpouring of the latter rain there was not the manifestation of the power of God there had been. We therefore went back to the regular order of work, expecting to spend more time in the evening, tarrying before the Lord. The boys went to their school work, and I went out to call on some people to talk to them about the gospel.

Our morning prayer meeting began at about half past seven. As usual, we all prayed at the same time, and each went out when he pleased. Upon returning at twelve o'clock, I heard some one praying in the prayer room. Going in to see who it was, I found our quietest and most timid boy, Wang Gia Swen, a boy of about eight years of age, hidden behind the organ praying in a loud voice and weeping as he confessed his sins to the Lord. He had been praying continuously since the morning service without stopping for breakfast.

As I came out of the prayer room the boys came out from their school. They were then to go to the garden or to the other kinds of industrial work for the rest of the day, but some of them wanted to know if they could stay to pray. Having been told that those who wished to might remain and pray; a few went to work, and all the others went into the prayer room and began praying. Almost at once there was another mighty outpouring of the Holy Spirit. This outpouring was so continuous that for over a week no more attempts were made to do regular work. We did only necessary things. Every one spent the rest of the time taking in the great blessings from God.

In the first days no one paid much attention to eating or sleeping. Whenever the young folks began to pray the power of God would fall, prostrating many to the floor. It was impossible to have meals at regular hours without interfering with the work of the Holy Spirit. After the power of God lifted from different ones they would go out for a time to rest or to take some food and then return to the prayer rooms soon to be under the power of the Holy Spirit again. These manifestations of the Spirit were so continuous that nearly all day until late in the night some were under His power. When things became quieter at nine or ten in the evenings, we would suggest that all go to bed and rest until the next morning. Usually several would want to pray and wait on the Lord longer. As these continued in prayer nearly all who had gone to bed would get up and return to pray. During these nights there was not much sleeping. Some of the boys never left the prayer rooms all night. They did not want to sleep. When they got sleepy they rested on the floor awhile and then got up to seek the Lord again. Soon they were lost once more in the things of God.

One thing is certain. This was a Holy Spirit outpouring that demanded nothing on the part of us missionaries except our keeping out of the way taking care not to interfere with His wonderful work. Our part was to open up our own hearts that we, too, might be taken deeper into the heavenly blessings that were falling in such mighty showers.

Our presence or absence in the meetings made little difference. One of the first mornings we were delayed in getting downstairs. Without any call to prayer meeting, one after another of the children had gone into the prayer rooms and begun praying and praising the Lord. When at last we were able to get past the many interruptions and go down to the prayer rooms we found several of the younger children prostrated under the power of the Holy Spirit and singing in other tongues as the Spirit gave them utterance.

From the very beginning the manifestations of the Spirit, the visions, and the revelations carried everything into the supernatural realm so far beyond our own limited knowledge or experience of supernatural matters that Mrs. Baker and I confessed to each other that these things had already passed to the place where the only resource we had was to believe that God was bigger than the devil. We took refuge behind the promise of God that we had before found safe, the promise that those who sought the Father for bread would not get a stone; those who sought a fish would not get a serpent; those who sought an egg would not get a scorpion; those who with pure motives, like these children, sought the Holy Spirit would not get evil things or demons, but would get exactly what they sought, the Holy Spirit (Luke 11:13).

In all the succeeding weeks God proved that promise true. Since He had proven that promise to us before, it set us free from anxiety as we saw and heard the wonderful things of God that took place in our midst, every day different, one wonder succeeded by another, as our wonder working God took His Adullam refugees from stage to stage and from glory to glory in His school of the Holy Spirit.

CHAPTER 2

SUPERNATURAL MANIFESTATIONS OF THE HOLY SPIRIT

MANY OF THE MOST MARVELOUS manifestations of the Holy Spirit were given to those who knew little of the Bible teaching on the subject, thus confirming the supernatural nature of these visions and confirming the reality of the outpourings of the Holy Spirit recorded in the New Testament.

Some children who had never heard us speak of the present day outpouring of the Holy Spirit as "the latter rain" in this outpouring upon Adullam actually experienced it as...

The Latter Rain.

As we all prayed and praised the Lord together with closed eyes some of the children seemed to feel water drop ping upon their heads. They were so busy seeking the Lord they did not want to hinder the blessing by opening their eyes to look around. At the same time, in their hearts they wondered how it could be sprinkling rain on them when there was a roof and a floor between them and the sky. But with the sprinkling their hearts were refreshed. As the dropping of water seemed to increase and the sprinkling became a shower it all seemed so glorious that the wonder of how it could rain in a downstairs room was forgotten. The sprinkling became a shower, the shower became a great downpour, the downpour became a deluge filling the room and rising higher and higher until the fortunate seeker was submerged in this wonderful life-giving flood from heaven.

At different times several children experienced this sense of the downpouring of rain. Six months after the great outpouring, and after a "dry spell," the flood gates of heaven were opened again, and there was another down pouring of the Holy Spirit. Again two of the small children experienced rain, "the latter rain," that seemed to fall upon their heads, penetrating and flooding their whole beings.

Through Bible study and through direct revelation by the Holy Spirit, Adullam is now coming to understand the meaning of this "rain." They understand that "this is that" spoken of by Joel the prophet: "He hath given you the former rain moderately, and he will cause to come down for you the rain, the former rain, and the latter rain in the first month" (Joel 2 :23).

The "former rain" was upon the first church, the seed church, sown on the earth on the day of Pentecost and the succeeding two or three hundred years. The "former rain" was the rain in the autumn upon the grain that was sown in the ground. Then came "the great falling way,"4 the long winter of the dark ages, the grain sown in the earth—the Church in the world—apparently dead. Then came sprinklings of the "latter rain" in the first month in the spring through Luther, Wesley, Fox, Finney, Moody, and other servants of God. Salvation by faith, the born again experience, holy living, first the blade and then the ear, began to come forth. Now the sprinkling is becoming a shower. Healing through faith in Jesus has come again. The Lord is again casting out devils, healing the sick, raising the dead, proving Himself the Almighty God in the midst of those who believe Him. The hope of the Coming King has revived. The Lord is again baptizing believers with the Holy Spirit as in the beginning, the former rain, so that they speak with other languages and prophesy as the Holy Spirit gives utterance (Acts 2 :4) .

The harvest is near. "The former rain," "the seed rain" (Rotherham), came moderately; "the latter rain," "the harvest rain" (Rotherham) will come abundantly to ripen the grain, to perfect the Church. There will be deluges of rain, the latter rain of the Holy Spirit. The greatest revival the world has ever seen is just ahead. The greatest miracles, the most wonderful wonder-working Church the world has ever seen is near. The downpouring of latter rain is at hand; the clouds are now filling the sky. According to promise the Lord will soon pour out his "Spirit upon all flesh." The church that was sown in the time of the "former rain" and fell into the earth and died has come forth. It will soon be the full corn in the ear. Beyond anything Pentecostal days ever saw, "Your sons and your daughters shall prophesy, your young men shall see visions," "and also upon the servants and upon the handmaidens in these days will I pour out of my spirit" (Joel 2:28, 29; Acts 2:17-21).

Because of this final and greatest outpouring of the Holy Spirit, the church in the full ear will have restored to it the years eaten by the locust, the canker-worm, the caterpiller, and the palmer worm (Joel 2:25). The fruits and gifts of the Holy Spirit will all be restored to the true church of bloodwashed believers. In its supernatural life and supernatural ministry, multitudes will be converted: "The floors shall be full of wheat and the vats shall over flow" (Joel 2:24); multitudes which no man can number will come into the garner "from all nations and kindreds and peoples and tongues" (Rev. 7:9).

If you read Acts 2 you will see that this outpouring upon "all flesh" is for to-day. Our Adullam people, at any rate, are sure of this. Many times has the Lord stood in their midst, made to them the same promises He made to first believers, and commissioned them with the same commission to carry the same gospel in the same power with which He sent forth the first disciples in the days of the "former rain." We know that "the latter rain" that fell on Adullam is like the former rain, but it is the last rain that will bring the wheat and tares to full harvest and separation and will usher in the return of the Lord of the harvest to gather the wheat into his barns and burn the tares in the furnace of fire.

The Holy Spirit has on different occasions and by different Adullam people been seen as a...

Tongue of Fire

upon the head of each one in the room. In some instances more than one person has seen this vision at the same time. Of course, all who are familiar with the Bible know that the things of God are not equally revealed to all.

When the Spirit has fallen in our meetings many have felt...

The Holy Spirit as a Wind

blowing upon them, flooding their souls with peace and power. These breezes from heaven have sometimes been in such power that we have no difficulty in believing the record that when the first disciples met together and "lifted up their voices to God with one accord, when they had prayed, the place was shaken where they were assembled together, and they were all filled with the Holy Ghost."7

Many times have older and younger children seen...

The Holy Spirit As Seven Lamps.

At times of special outpouring of the Holy Spirit these seven lamps of fire were seen let down from heaven into the room in our very midst. At other times in the visions of the throne of Christ in heaven, children saw the "seven lamps of fire burning before the throne, which are the seven Spirits of God" (Rev. 4:5). We all knew that the seven lamps meant the Holy Spirit in our midst.

In the first days of the outpouring of the Spirit one small boy spoke in pure prophecy when in the Spirit he seemed to be in heaven at the feet of Jesus. The Lord spoke through him in the first person clearing up many things the children did not understand and telling them how to tarry and how to seek the Spirit. At that time the Lord said, "When the Spirit is in your midst do not open your eyes, for that will hinder; the Holy Spirit will descend to give you power to preach the gospel, to cast out demons, and to heal the sick; the Holy Spirit is in seven colors, red, blue, and other colors." One of the older boys then said that when the Spirit had been upon him he had seen a great, red light and other colors. The word from the Lord explained this to him and others who had seen different colors. Of course I know light is made up of seven colors but I had never thought of the seven lamps before the throne of God, the Holy Spirit, as seven colors. All light comes from God, and God is light.

These Adullam people have also seen…

The Holy Spirit Brighter Than the Noon-Day Sun

This manifestation of the Holy Spirit as a great light has been very common. Some children, having opened their eyes to see if it was something about the electric light, could scarcely discern the lights in the room because of the exceeding glory of the light of heaven which seemed to fill the place. These children know what Paul meant when he said that on the Damascus road the light that shone about him was "a light from heaven" that was "brighter than the noon-day sun" (Acts 26:13). After their visions of heaven and this great light brighter and clearer than any they had seen on earth Adullam people know why in heaven "there shall be no night; and they need no candle, neither light of the sun; for the Lord God giveth them light." Through these manifestations and revelations these one-time-beggar children in this dark land on this dark earth know beyond a doubt that in the New Jerusalem in heaven "the city has no need of the sun, neither of the moon to shine in it; for the glory of God lightens it and the lamb is the light thereof" (Rev. 21:23).

CHAPTER 3

SCRIPTURAL RESULTS OF THE OUTPOURING

THAT THIS OUTPOURING of the Holy Spirit is from God can be clearly seen in that it exactly fulfils the prophecies in the Bible that foretell what results will follow outpourings of the Holy Spirit. We mention some of these results. One of these that was to accompany the work of the Holy Spirit and that was first manifest among us was a...

Clear Assurance of Salvation.

Through visions or other workings of the Holy Spirit, sin and the lost condition of each one was made so real that every ground of hope was banished unless the Lord in undeserved mercy would answer prayer for the lost and save him. Then the Holy Spirit made the wonderful salvation and grace of God as real as had been the lost condition. One after another soon came through to a clear "I know" experience of salvation. This made such a transformation in the lives and testimony of the

Adullam family that there was no mistaking that the Home was made up of many who were...

Born Again.

The whole atmosphere of the place was changed. The joy unspeakable and full of glory came in until it bubbled over. As the boys were at their work in opening ground for a garden they praised the Lord so much that some of the boys in the neighborhood, mocking them said, "Praise the Lord," whenever they met our boys. When one boy went into a store to buy nails, before he realized it he said, "Hallelujah! I want some nails." The tribes boy has had a wonderful experience from the start. One day on his way to work he danced down the street in the joy of the Holy Spirit, praising the Lord somewhat like the style of Billy Bray. Being cleansed from sin and born again of the Holy Spirit and still seeking more and more of the Lord, the children were carried into these deeper things of God until over twenty of the Adullam people...

Spoke in Other Tongues

as people did on the day of Pentecost; as they did when the Holy Spirit was poured forth at the House of Cornelius; as they did when they received the fulness of the Spirit at Ephesus; as the apostle Paul did; and as the Samaritan Christians undoubtedly did when they received the Holy Spirit in mysterious power and manifestation, so striking and wonderful that Simon wanted to buy it.

Although most of these Adullam people had never seen any such demonstrations, having been taught to seek the Lord for the Holy Spirit, they were not only rewarded with a great "joy unspeakable and full of glory" in their own hearts, but they got the "I know" satisfaction about the baptism of the Holy Spirit.

They know they received it the same way the New Testament saints did in the beginning, as shown by the only five recorded passages of scripture just mentioned which tell how the apostles and first disciples received the Holy Spirit and what they did when they were fully immersed, or baptized, in the supernatural Spirit.9 These Chinese boys and girls were saved by the same Lord and baptized with the same Holy Spirit in the same way as the first disciples, for like them, they not only spoke with other tongues but also…

Prophesied as the Spirit Gave Them Utterance.

No one present at the time has ever doubted that the Lord spoke to us by direct inspiration in the first days of the outpouring of the Spirit when He spoke through one of the smallest and humblest of the children. There was something about the voice, the penetrating power of those words, a heart-gripping power that cannot be described. We had never heard such a gripping voice from God in any sermon in all our days. We all knew we were hearing directly from the Lord. Quite a number of the Adullam people later spoke in prophecy, insomuch that we marvelled more and more at the miracles that were taking place as the Lord spoke the wonderful things of God, revealing His plans and purposes in picking the outcast "nothings" of the earth, who were recent beggar boys, to make them the mouthpieces of the living God, speaking through them by direct inspiration, edifying and building up this little group of simple blood-washed believers so recently saved out of hopeless physical and spiritual despair.

Another most striking result of the work of the Holy Spirit was the way in which, according to the Word, He fulfilled the promise that when He, the Comforter, came He would take of the things of Christ to show to His disciples and would show them "things to come."10

It seemed most wonderful how the Spirit revealed to these

simple believers, who had only heard of the Bible for a few months, the things of Christ, His salvation, and the things of the future by…

Visions of the Unseen Worlds.

Many of these visions were given to several at the same time. Nearly all of the visions were seen by quite a number of persons. In many cases the children came to ask if the Bible said anything about certain things they had seen in vision.11

The visions, seen by even some of the smallest children six years of age, as well as by the older boys, were seen while they were under the Power of the Holy Spirit, not as a dream but as real life.

Some of the visions seen were: Christ tied to a post and scourged; Christ bleeding on the cross while scoffers looked on; the body of Christ taken from the cross, carried to the tomb, placed in the tomb, and the tomb closed; an angel opening the tomb and Christ's resurrection; His appearance to the women, to the disciples by the sea, and to those in the upper room; the ascension of Christ and the descent of the two angels; heaven; detailed visions inside the New Jerusalem in heaven; angels; the redeemed; hell; the condition of the lost in hell; demons; the devil; the great tribulation and things pertaining to saints and to the subjects of the beast during that time; the battle of Armageddon; the binding and imprisonment of Satan in the pit; the binding of the Anti-Christ; the devil cast out of heaven; the Great Supper of God and birds eating flesh of kings and captains of the earth; the coming of Christ with his angels; the sun and moon changed; heaven quake and earth quake and destruction that attended the coming of Christ; the resurrection of the righteous; the marriage supper of the Lamb in Paradise; detailed views of our mansions in heaven and other heavenly scenes.

This work of the Holy Spirit through visions, as well as in the heart, created such a great interest in...

Bible Study

that even the smaller children wanted to know if they could stop studying "earthly books" and study the Bible only.

Since the unseen world became so real, it is no wonder that there was a change in the life of...

Prayer and Praise.

While not all the Adullam people spoke in other tongues, all except those who were too dull of mind to understand much of anything were anointed and filled with the Holy Spirit in a much greater measure than ever before, so that Adullam was often lifted up to heavenly places in Christ to joyfully praise and worship the King. Although there were times when a person almost wondered if these heavenly citizens would come "down to earth" again, there was no need to fear. This any one would have seen who could have been in one prayer meeting where boy after boy in real intercessory prayer pleaded with God for the lost, praying that God would use us all as real warriors for Him in this battle of righteousness. The experiences already related have made prayer more than a formality. All know now that our foes are spiritual hosts of wickedness in heavenly places.

Preach in the Power of the Holy Spirit

After two or three weeks of the Lord's dealing with them, nearly all the children wanted to preach, even the younger ones. There was some real preaching in the power and demonstration of the Holy Spirit. Some of both the younger and older boys hardly seemed like our boys when they preached under the real unction of the Holy Spirit, not timidly and apologetically as before, but as having authority. Hell and heaven, the devil and his power, Christ, His blood, and His salvation, were no myths to these boys. They knew the Lord told them to preach, and they were given the message, "Repent, for the Kingdom of heaven is at hand." As we listened to some of these messages preached with great assurance, warning people to flee from the wrath to come and showing them the wonderful salvation in the love of Christ, our hearts rejoiced within us. When the Power of God was especially great in our midst there was some unusually miraculous preaching.

At the Chinese New Year, when the streets were filled with all classes of people out for a holiday, we Adullam people, having circulated thousands of tracts, formed a circle on the street to preach the gospel.

One of the older boys had prepared a sermon on a New Year theme. But when the preaching began, the power of God so fell that this boy suddenly began speaking in other tongues, while another person interpreted. One small boy after another preached as interpreter. As soon as the Lord was through with one interpreter he would step back and another feel the unction to preach. As soon as this one stepped into the circle he would get the interpretation. This went on for an hour or two while as many people listened as could get near enough to hear. There were some people of the type that seldom listen to the gospel who now listened most attentively as these boys spoke with an earnestness that must have seemed strange and unusual. As we came away from that service conducted by the Holy Spirit in such order and beauty, each preacher being of the Lord's appointment, each one speaking the message from Him under direct inspiration, we could but ponder in our hearts at these wonders of God. We seemed to see something of what the preaching of the church was in the beginning and what it seemed so clear the Lord wanted it to be in the end.

Not that preaching through other tongues and interpretation

was in the beginning or subsequently to be the regular order of preaching, but, as I Cor. chapter 14 clearly shows, such preaching constitutes a part of the Lord's method of preaching the Gospel in the power and demonstration of the Holy Spirit.

In such preaching the mind of the speaker is entirely inactive, and before utterance he does not know what words the Spirit will speak through his lips. This is pure prophetic preaching.

In the preaching of the gospel to the nations of the earth and in the building up of believers in the church the mind of the speaker may be active and know, at least momentarily, before utterance what the Spirit will speak through him. The message may be an exposition of the Scriptures, as in the sermon by Stephen, or otherwise. Peter on various occasions "being filled with the Holy Spirit preached as the Spirit gave him utterance."

Although preaching the gospel under the direct unction of the Holy Spirit is not exactly pure prophecy, it is nevertheless, prophetic when definitely guided and directed by the Holy Spirit.

There were a few other instances of preaching with tongues and interpretation in some of the villages.

The Lord was the preacher on several occasions in our little street chapel. For two or three nights the youthful preachers, under the real unction of the Spirit, preached the most inspiring sermons I have ever heard from Chinese evangelists. It seemed as if those sermons would stir any one to real repentance. God showed his love in still greater power a few nights later. When a boy in his teens was preaching with real power his eyes suddenly closed and he began to...

Prophesy like an Old Testament Prophet

under direct inspiration of the Holy Spirit in pure prophecy. The manner of the preacher suddenly changed; the form of the Chinese sentences became rhythmic and perfect; the address changed to the first person, such as, "I am the Lord God

Almighty, the one true God, who made all things, who now speaks to you through this boy." "Against me have you sinned." The penetrating words, the sense of having been ushered into the presence of God, I cannot describe. The seats of our little chapel were soon filled, while as many people as could see gathered about the door, listening in awe and wonder. If there was the least commotion the Lord commanded order, speaking through that boy and saying, "Make no mistake in this matter. Listen carefully and understand. I the Lord God, have all the authority in heaven and on earth. To me every man and every demon must give account. I know all about every one of you. I know all your sins. I know how many hairs are on your head. There are fifty-six of you living in sin here to-night. Repent to-night, and I'll forgive you." For half an hour or more we verily were in the presence of a prophet, as the Lord in this way rebuked those people for idolatry, ungodliness, and all their vices, until there was no ground for hope left anywhere. Then, as in the case of the Old Testament prophets, God spake of the glories He had prepared for His people. Like a loving father he pleaded with them to repent that night. He spoke of the coming of distress upon the nations and of the destruction of this ungodly race in the day of God's wrath. All these things were repeated several times with exhortations to listen to every word as from a God who would hold every person present accountable for his own soul after that night.

When the prophecy was finished the boy sat down. There was not a move or a whisper. It seemed to me that every person must know that God was speaking. Nearly all present had come in while the boy's eyes were shut. When the Lord spoke saying there were fifty-six present bound by the devil and sin, one of the boys carefully counted those not of our own Christian boys. There were just fifty-six.12

A striking instance was that of a man from whom…

Two Demons Were Cast Out.

The Lord had told the boys through prophecy and direct revelation, "Demons must obey me." They saw the Lord prove His word. Had we space to give details, we could prove beyond any other possible explanation that actual living demons were cast out of one devil-possessed man. It would take too long to give the history of this man. We had known him a number of years, and he has since been with us six months. In short, he had been, for many years, the victim of melancholy. Because he was so bound in chains of darkness that he was ready to take his own life we had kept him with us to prevent this. He was always sad. All effort to lead him to any knowledge of salvation through Christ was of no avail. His mind was blind to everything pertaining to the blood.

The Lord used three people in casting out the demons. One demon the size of a man had an awful, black appearance. Several children saw him come out. While being rebuked through the Lord's using one suddenly "filled with the Holy Spirit" for the particular occasion, the demons put up a final fight for the man of their possession. The man's hands clenched together; his eyes shut tight; his whole body became rigid and resisting.

Finally the Holy Spirit enlightened the man's heart; his body relaxed; his hands went up to God in praise.

Angry Demon Grabs School Teacher

Several children saw the demon after he came out, rushing about in great anger, seeking whom he might enter or tear.14 All the children having rushed in from where they had just sat down to their meal, stood about with uplifted hands, thanking and praising Jesus. Among these the demon saw no opportunity, for they were all looking to Jesus whose blood covered them. The school teacher, who was not truly converted, also came in and was looking on in curiosity but was not praying. The angry demon, seeing his opportunity, seized this man and threw him to the floor with a thud. There the second demon sat upon him, so that the teacher could not rise. Several children saw this. Our gardener, who was some years ago miraculously delivered from opium, saw this too. He was suddenly filled with the Holy Spirit and cast the demon out of the room.

I saw only the two men, the one unbound and set free, the other suddenly fall beside him. I supposed the school teacher was prostrated by the Holy Spirit of God that was present in great power. I questioned him when he was able to arise as to why he wept and why he fell. He said, "I wept from sheer terror. Something awful happened. Every thing became black; I saw myself about to go into a black pit at the base of a terrible mountain." When on the floor, he saw himself being bound by demon chains and about to be carried off into terrorizing darkness, but he was set free again.

The physical appearance of the man from whom demons were cast out changed at once. He testified that he had peace and joy in his heart. He was given a vision of heaven at the time he was delivered from demons. When he lay in bed in the evening thinking about the Lord he got so happy that he wondered if it was right for him to have such great joy.

CHAPTER 4

VISIONS OF HEAVEN

THE BIBLE TELLS US THE HEAVEN of the redeemed is "the third heaven."15 The future home of the people of the Lord is a **place** in the third heaven. This **place** is a **city**. The name of this city is "The New Jerusalem." This New Jerusalem is not "a figure of speech." It is not a combination of ideas skillfully clothed in earthly words of the Lord to give man a false conception of something it is not. The Bible says this New Jerusalem is a real city with a real foundation which God himself laid.

This celestial city is foursquare, one thousand five hundred miles on every side, surrounded by a wall two hundred feet high with foundations of twelve kinds of precious stones, the most beautiful precious stones known to man. The wall itself is jasper, which sends forth a brilliant jasper light. Twelve gates lead into the city, the streets of which are like burnished gold.16

In this city are the homes of the redeemed, the abode of angels, Paradise, and the throne of God.

Why should not the New Jerusalem be a real city with streets of real gold and with jasper walls and with foundation stones of precious jewels? Did God so exhaust his material when he made the universe that he had no gold or jewels left for heaven? If God could make a world, could he not suspend a city in the sky beyond the stars? Here and there a little impure gold in a fissure of a distorted rock of this cursed and perverted earth or here and there the discovery of a precious jewel hidden in the debris of earthly ruins are only lingering reminders of the reality of which these are merely shadows. The real, the imperishable are in the city whose builder and maker is God.

What we see on this perverted, degenerated earth are only **shadows**. "The creation fell into subjection to failure and **unreality**" (Rom. 8:20) . The gold we cherish, the jewels we adore, the cities and mansions we build are only copies of the real in the city that is soon coming down.

The Adullam children were caught up in vision to this city of God. How they could see the city I do not know. **How** Abraham saw it I do not know. **How** Paul could be caught up to Paradise, either in the body or out of the body, I do not know. These things are beyond natural order. We need not, at present, know the **How**. We know the **Fact**. John was shown the city. He was told by the Lord to write the things he had seen and send them to the Churches.

In the Spirit Adullam children were caught up to this city time after time, not as in a dream but as a living reality. Their visits were so real, in fact, that the children supposed their souls actually left their bodies to go to heaven and return, or that in some unaccountable way they had gone to heaven soul and body just as they might in daily life visit some distant place. Frequently when in Paradise the children were plucking and partaking of the heavenly fruit, they gathered some extra to tuck in their garments to bring back to earth for "Muh Si and Si Mu" (Pastor and Mrs. Baker).

They knew they were only on a visit to heaven and soon to return. Upon returning, when the Spirit lifted from them, finding themselves in our Adullam rooms they proceeded at once to search in their garments for the delicious fruit they had brought back to please us. Not finding this fruit in their garments, a look of great surprise, confusion, and disappointment came over their faces. They could not, for the time, believe they had not bodily gone to heaven and come back with the fruit tucked in their garments.

Walking on the streets of the New Jerusalem was to them as real as walking on the streets of a Chinese city. One day, when walking down the street in bright sunshine, I asked the boys if the visions were as real and as clear as what we then saw. "Just as real," they said, "but much clearer due to the light in heaven and the white garments and the cleanliness everywhere, all adding to the brightness."

When in the Spirit, the children were usually lost to their natural surroundings. In many cases, although they supposed they were in heaven, they talked aloud, describing what they saw, thus carrying on conversation that we all could hear. Often they acted out before our eyes what they supposed they were doing in heaven.

Caught up to the Third Heaven

The Adullam children said they went to the third heaven. As they passed through the first heaven they felt air on their faces. Having passed the second heaven, they looked back upon the stars in their wonderful beauty, much as from a mountain height a person might gaze down upon a beautiful, light-studded city below. From this starry heaven they passed on into the third heaven until they...

Came to the Heavenly Jerusalem.

As they approached this heavenly city they saw its light in the distance. Coming nearer, they saw the beautiful wall radiating its wonderful jasper light. The foundations were of indescribable beauty, sparkling with red, yellow, orange, purple, blue, green, violet, and all the other colors of the twelve most beautiful jewels.

This city in the sky the children saw as three cities in one: one city suspended above another, the largest city below, the smallest city on top, making a pyramid. Since this city John saw is surrounded by a wall, and since the city is one thousand five hundred miles high, Bible students have supposed the heavenly city is not a cube but a pyramid. Our children, however, knew nothing of this, neither had I ever thought of the New Jerusalem as three cities, one suspended above another. God who suspends the worlds in space can suspend these cities in space. The Bible does not tell us the internal order of the city.17

One of our small boys spoke in prophecy when in vision at the feet of the Lord, the Lord was talking to him. In this prophecy the Lord said that he had made heaven big enough for everybody, that he had made it in three cities one above another, and that at present his throne is in the upper city.

Since time and distance are nothing in the heavenly realm, there is nothing impossible in such an arrangement of this city of God. There are three heavens. There were three stories in the ark, where God preserved the present creation. God is three in one. Why should not the city of the Great King be three in one? Why should not the King reign from the top of the pyramid of all the universe, since "the stone which the builders rejected was made the head of the corner," the capstone of the pyramid of all creation?

By the Gates into the City

Adullam entered by its pearly gates into the city of golden streets. Angels in white guarded the gates and welcomed those entering in. No beggarly reception this. Here the one-time rejected off-scourings of the earth were welcomed as kings by these angelic hosts. Had not the Savior promised the weakest and humblest of his children a kingdom where they shall reign with the King of Kings for ages and ages?

Through the gates into the city! Out of earth into heaven! Out of the mortal into the immortal! Out of death into life! All the old life behind and below! All the new life ahead and above! Inside the gates! Angels, angels every where. Angels talking, angels singing, angels rejoicing, angels playing harps and blowing trumpets, angels dancing and praising the King. Such a scene no mortal ever saw; such floods of inner joy flooded the whole being as no one ever knew except when filled with the Holy Spirit, the eternal life, the heavenly life of God, "the earnest," "down payment" of heaven.

The children clapped their hands in rapture. They shouted for joy. They sometimes rolled on the floor in unrestrained laughter and jumped and danced in great delight, while their faces were so transformed by this heavenly joy that the glory of the celestial city seemed to shine upon us. There was no sorrow in this city; no mournful, long-faced religion there; no funeral dirges in the hymns. This was a city of joy, "joy in the Holy Spirit," "joy unspeakable and full of glory."

With Innumerable Hosts of Angels

Inside the city, the children knew the meaning of the Scripture which says, "Ye are come into the city of the living God, the heavenly Jerusalem, and to innumerable hosts of angels" (Heb. 12 :22) . Not only about the gates of the city were these happy angels, but also throughout the city everywhere were these heavenly hosts. Angels were always ready to escort the children from place to place throughout the city; angels walked with them and talked with them; angels explained to them the meaning of things they did not understand, even as they talked with John and revealed to him the things of God.

Often in these experiences with the angels our children were given harps and taught to play them and sing as the angels did. They were also taught to blow the trumpets and were taught…

The Music and Language of Heaven.

When we saw the children, with closed eyes, all dancing about the room in rhythm, we found that in vision they were dancing with the angels in heaven and keeping time to the heavenly music. When we saw them apparently blowing a trumpet or going through the motions of playing a harp, we found that in vision they were joining the heavenly orchestra in the praises of the King. We could not see the heavenly harps or trumpets. We could not see the angels' joyful dance or hear their song. We could hear only the children singing heavenly songs. It was a daily sight to find some child off in a corner by himself, lying comfortably on the pine needles, going through the motions of playing a harp. Upon going near, we could hear him singing a new song we had never taught him. Approaching still nearer, we would discover that the words were as strange to us as the tune. The singer was singing in the **heavenly choir**. His song was the song the angels taught him. The words of the song must have been in the language of angels.[20] Seeing the children singing in this heavenly angelic choir was a sight not to be forgotten. Sometimes several of them in some place in the heavenly city or its wonderful Paradise would decide to play and sing together. With closed eyes, while fully under the power of the Holy Spirit, three or four of them would get off by themselves. If we were near, we would hear a consultation as to who would play the trumpet and who would sing. After all was decided and everybody was ready, the heavenly hymns began. The trumpeters held their hands up before them and blew as though blowing trumpets. The harpists both played and sang, while those without instruments joined in the singing. In these cases they always sang in languages we did not understand, unless by mutual agreement they decided to sing one of those hymns they "used to sing down on earth." In that case they sang in Chinese.

Seeing and Worshipping Jesus

The climax of all heavenly joy and wonder was "seeing Jesus" and worshipping Him who had saved them by His blood.

Soon after entering the gates of the city the children were escorted by the angels to "go and see Jesus." We could hear these children talking about "going to see Jesus" and see them as in vision they were approaching the throne of Christ. When they came into the wonderful presence they stood reverently gazing with love and devotion upon the Lord of all creation, who was also their Savior. First of all they thanked Him, and adoringly worshipping Him they joined their hands before them, bowing in true obeisance. Then they knelt and bowed their faces to the floor in true worship "in spirit and truth,"[21] which few if any know on earth who have not the baptism of God's Holy Spirit.

The Throne of God and the Throne of Christ

The throne of Christ the children saw as did John when he was "in the Spirit": "And behold there was a throne set in heaven, and one sitting upon the throne; and he that sat was to look upon like a jasper stone and a sardius: and there was a rainbow round about the throne, like an emerald to look upon. And round about the throne were four and twenty thrones: and upon the thrones I saw four and twenty elders sitting arrayed in white garments: and on their heads crowns of gold,—and there were seven lamps of fire burning before the throne, which are the seven Spirits of God." Rev. 4:3-6.

Jesus Preeminent in all Things in Heaven

No matter how amazed were the children at the wonders of the golden city, no matter how happy in the pleasures of Paradise, no matter how joyful in the presence of the angels, Jesus was never forgotten. His name was mentioned in all the conversation; his praise was mingled in all the enjoyments; he was always magnified everywhere, in everything, and in everybody there.

Houses by the Golden Street

On either side of the beautiful golden streets were buildings side by side, a room for each person, every room opening onto the street. Upon the door and about the front were precious jewels so resplendently brilliant that the building shone with light and glory. The name of each occupant was above the door. Angels led the children into the rooms. Within all the rooms were the same kinds of furnishings: a beautiful golden table upon which was a Bible, a flower vase, a pen, and a book; by the table was a golden chair; there was also a wonderful golden chest and a golden bed. In each room was a jewelled crown, a golden harp, and a trumpet. The walls were gold. From the Bible, made of such paper as had never been seen on earth and bound with gold, light and such brilliant glory shone forth that the whole room needed no other light. The visitors were told that when they came to stay after death they could go out into Paradise and pick any flowers of their choice to place in the beautiful vase on the golden table.23

In these visits to heaven the children could go to their rooms at pleasure to read their Bibles or to play their harps and trumpets. Sometimes they took their trumpets or harps out into the streets or out into Paradise to play and sing with the angels and the redeemed who are now in heaven.

In these excursions through heaven the children, though lost to their real surroundings on earth, were always conscious that their visit to heaven was temporary. They knew they were there only to see what was prepared for them after death, so they might go back to earth again to tell others. Angels and the Lord told these heavenly visitors that, if they believed and obeyed, all these things would be theirs. They not only knew they must come back to earth again, but they sometimes knew when they were coming.

One boy, after enjoying the glories of heaven, hung his crown and trumpet up in his room so he could have them again after he died and went to heaven to remain. He then came back to earth. The power of the Holy Spirit left him. When he opened his eyes he was in our Adullam room telling the wonders of his trip to heaven.

Can we suppose the Lord saved these boys, baptized them with the Holy Spirit, and then fooled them by showing them a figurative and mythical heaven? Impossible!!! An earthly father may deceive his children with false hopes and false promises. Our Heavenly Father shows his children what he has for them (I Cor. 2:10), promises he will give these things (Rev. 3:21), and then gives the very things which He has promised (Lu. 11:9, 13).

When these children saw the heavenly rooms of their Adullam friends they clapped their hands, laughed, and shouted with great joy, calling each one by name to come and see his room. The one in the Spirit was passing along the streets of the New Jerusalem, reading the names above each door.

In Heaven Meet Adullam Boys Who Died

The first day when the Holy Spirit fell upon the children, and one of the boys was caught up to heaven, with angels who came to welcome him came also the two Adullam boys who were undoubtedly saved and who died the year before. These two, "Hsi Dien Fu" and "Djang Hsing," had with them in heaven a little girl who died in Kotchiu four years previous, whom our children had forgotten.

These who had died and gone on before led those who were caught up in the joys and wonders of heaven. They led them to see Jesus, first of all, and to worship and thank Him. After this they were shown their dwellings and escorted around the city or led out into Paradise to play.

All who went to heaven were given white garments. The angels, also dressed in seamless garments of spotless white, had wings, but the redeemed did not have wings. There was a clear distinction between the two.

Later on many more of the children saw these Adullam boys who are in heaven. Heaven did not seem far away as, caught away in the Spirit, they acted out heavenly visions before our eyes. With closed eyes and radiant faces they clapped their hands and shouted for joy to these boys who died that year, calling them to hurry over to see some dwelling, some golden street, some new scene among the angels, some new discovery in the garden of Paradise, or to come and play the harp and sing with them the praises of Jesus. These boys who had died were so constantly seen in heaven and their names were so frequently shouted in our midst with ecstasy and joy that they did not seem far away— just out of sight. Heaven was so real, so near, so wonderful, so certain, that if one of our children had died in those days the others would have envied him his privilege.

The step to heaven after death or at the coming of the Lord seemed so small and the coming of the Lord so near that it removed from our minds all mystery as to why the first disciples could sell their possessions and face persecution and death without wavering.

Our kingdom is not of this world. Our citizenship is in heaven, whence also we wait for our Savior. Our life, our work, our service, our hardships here are only brief and passing incidents on the way to the true life, the true city, in the true kingdom that cannot be shaken.

CHAPTER 5

PARADISE

Scripture Teaches the Regeneration of Natural Creation

BEFORE TELLING ABOUT THE VISIONS of Paradise we wish to show that such a Paradise as these children saw is in accord with the Father's plans for his children, as revealed in his written word. When the Lord created the first perfect man and his perfect bride he "planted a garden eastward" in Eden, in which he put the man whom he had formed. "And out of the ground made Jehovah God to grow every tree that is pleasant to the sight, and good for food, the tree of life also in the midst of the garden" (Gen. 2:9). Hence, in the beginning, the Lord planned for man to dwell in the midst of all the beauties of nature. He was given a home in the garden in the eastern part of Eden, the wonder "park" that God himself planned and planted. In that order there was no sin. There was no sickness or death. There was no thorn or thistle. There was no curse. That was a different world from this. That world was a heaven on earth with man enjoying what might have been eternal life, in dominion over a whole world of trees and flowers "pleasant to

43

the sight," a whole world of beauty and glory such as the present earth has never seen. God planned all these things for man's eternal happiness.

When sin entered, man's enjoyment of this creation became a limited, temporal enjoyment. The first Creation of birds, and flowers, and trees, and animals, that were in the first world and its Eden in an eternal state, fell into a lower order that is not eternal. "For the creation fell into subjection to failure and unreality." Sin lost to man his Eden "park" and his Eden God.

Restored from sin, man will be restored to his Eden God and his Eden "park." But man will be restored to more than the primal order. He will be born again into the new spiritual order.

The first order was earthly; the last is spiritual but real. It is similar to the earthly, even as Christ after his resurrection was real and similar but still spiritual and different from the earthly order. He still could eat and drink with his disciples. He still had flesh and bones that could be felt and hands that could serve fish and bread to His hungry disciples. But in the resurrected order the Lord was not subject to the limitations of the material world of time, and space, and physical bounds. Even so the world with its natural order of animal, bird, and plant creation is to be born again into a higher, spiritual order similar to the first creation but also different from it. It will be the real order not again subject to corruption and unreality (Rom. 8:20, Weymouth).

The natural creation is to be born again through the resurrection of Christ. Christ saves more than man. He saves the whole creation that fell into unreality in the fall of man. For "all creation, gazing eagerly as if with outstretched neck, is waiting and longing to see the manifestation of the sons of God. There was always the hope that, at last, the creation itself would also be set free from the thraldom of decay, so as to enjoy the liberty that will attend the glory of the children of God" (Rom. 8 :19-21 Weymouth). If this does not mean that the present natural order of plant, animal, and all natural life looks forward to being set free in the same resurrected order and the same liberty the saved are to enjoy in a new estate, what does it mean? All nature looks forward to the new spiritual regeneration that belongs to the redeemed, for Christ "brought us forth by the word of truth, that we should be a kind of first fruits of His creatures."

Christ himself "is the image of the invisible God, the first-born of all creation." How is Christ "the first-born of all creation" unless it be that in his resurrection into the new order animal and plant creation will eventually follow in this order as the full harvest of which Christ was but the "first-fruits"? Even the earth itself is to be a regenerated in the new order, since "according to his promise we look for new heavens and a new earth, wherein dwelleth righteousness" (II Pet 3:13). Will not that new earth have trees and flowers and animals and birds and all the beauties of glorified nature in a higher incorruptible order that shall abide forever?

"The wolf also shall dwell with the lamb, and the leopard shall lie down with the kid; and the calf and the young lion and the fatling together; and a little child shall lead them" (Isa. 11:6).

These things are as certain as the word of God, for he that sitteth on the throne said, "Behold I make all things new," and He said, "Write for these words are faithful and true" (Rev. 21:5).

John "saw a new heaven and a new earth," and he also "saw the holy city, New Jerusalem, coming down out of heaven" to the New Earth.

As there was an Eden park of pleasure and fruits on the first earth so, also, in a higher, regenerated, resurrected order, the New Jerusalem will contain an Eden park on the New Earth in the new order. This Eden "park" is already in heaven in the New Jerusalem that has not yet descended, but is soon coming down.

Paradise is a "Park" of Plant, Animal, and Regenerated Nature

Perhaps the revelation of such a Paradise in heaven as Adullam saw will be as new to most of the readers as it was to us. This is because we are so dull of mind and slow of heart to "believe all that is written in the scriptures."

We did not teach these children about this Paradise. The children taught us. Some of the smallest children, who were naturally most ignorant of these matters, were our best teachers. That they got these things from the Lord is clearly evident, as you will see by a comparison with the teaching of the Bible. It teaches there is just such a Paradise in heaven as these children saw. Paul said he knew a man who was "caught up even to the third heaven" and that this person "was caught up into Paradise."29 In the messages of Revelation "the Spirit saith to the Churches, to him that overcometh, to him will I give to eat of the tree of life, which is in the Paradise of God" (Rev. 2:7). Of the heavenly scene we are also told that "on this side of the river and on that was the tree of life bearing twelve manner of fruits."30 Hence there is a Paradise in heaven with flowing water and trees of fruit.

This Paradise is a great "park" of surpassing wonder; that is just what the word "Paradise" means. "Paradise" means "Eden." "Eden" means "Paradise." "Eden" is a "park ;" "Paradise" is therefore a "park." Peloubet's Bible Dictionary says of "Paradise," "This is a word of Persian origin, and is used in the Septuagint as the translation of 'Eden.' It means an orchard of pleasure and fruits, a garden, or pleasure ground something like an English park." But this "park" in heaven is only "some thing like" a park on earth, because it is as much greater than earthly parks, in extent and beauty, as God's thoughts are greater than man's thoughts. Man's most beautiful parks, with their picturesque landscapes, their flowing streams, their crystal pools, the wooded nooks, the verdant greens, the fragrant, variegated flowers, the carolling birds, and animal pets, are only imperfect imitations on the part of man to reproduce the Eden that was "in the beginning."

If God did not put into the heart of man this love for nature and this desire for natural parks of pleasure and fruit, whence came this universal love of nature, that has been in the heart of man from the days of his earliest history? Is all man's efforts to preserve a little of the vanishing natural beauties of this cursed and perishing earth only a vain fancy to be followed for only a few fleeting years? Is a love for the birds, and animals, and flowers, and trees, and mountains, and valleys, and lakes, and streams, and all this handiwork of God just a passing amusement given by the Lord to cheer us a little on this pilgrim journey? Are not the finest combinations of all that is beautiful in nature just mere fore-shadows of the unperverted and unlimited realities in the Paradise of God in heaven?

These natural beauties are not just scenes passed on a pilgrim journey. They are guide ways of God, pointing to the Eden of beauty at the end of the way. Love of nature may become an eternal love, enlarged beyond all natural limits for all who overcome by the blood of the Lamb, who, by faith in him, enter by the gates into the city with its Paradise of God, the Eden park in heaven whose beauty sin will never mar.

Adullam Children See Paradise, the Heaven Park

You will be interested, as we were, in what our Adullam children saw in the Paradise, the Eden, in the city beyond the sky. One of the young men was in Paradise almost as soon as he entered the heavenly city. There he was met by the two Adullam boys who had died in Hokow. These boys, taking him through Paradise and the other parts of the Holy City, soon came to a great, lawn like, grassy, open plot surrounded by magnificent trees, golden and sparkling.

The whole scene was so entrancing the young man said to his two glorified friends, "This is good enough for me. There cannot be anything more beautiful. I will stay right here." The boys who had preceded him to heaven said, "No, do not wait here, for there are much greater marvels." Going on a little farther they came to still more wonderful trees, some of them bearing fruit. The whole park-like surrounding and the grassy lawn beneath the trees were enticing beyond any earthly understanding. The young man said, "I must stay here, I cannot go on and leave this great beauty. I am so happy." "Come on," said the others, "there are many things in heaven exceeding this." "You go," he replied, "but I shall remain right here for awhile." The others left him on the grass under the trees with the great, open, velvet-like grassy space before him. Floods of joy and happiness he had never known on earth flooded his whole being. He was in the land of joy, "joy unspeakable and full of glory," "the land that is fairer than day."

Frequently an angel came walking by, playing a harp and singing. The angel smiled, offered him the harp. "I cannot play," he said. The angel passed by. Soon other angels came, smiling to him as they played and sang.

The angels were dressed in seamless garments of white; their faces were perfect; one was not more beautiful than another. "When they smiled—Oh, I can't describe that," the boy said, "there is no way on earth to describe the angels' smile."

Similar and surpassing beautiful scenes in Paradise were seen, repeatedly seen, by a large number of Adullam children. In Paradise they saw trees bearing the most delicious fruit, and vistas of most beautiful flowers of every color and hue, sending forth an aroma of surpassing fragrance. There were birds of glorious plumage singing their carols of joy and praise. In this park were also animals of every size and description: large deer, small deer, large lions, great elephants, lovely rabbits, and all sorts of little friendly pets such as they had never seen before.

Playing with the Lion and Other Animals in the Heaven Paradise Park

The children held the little pets in their arms and passed

them from one to another. Or perhaps they found the lion peacefully lying beneath a tree. In that case they climbed on his back, ran their fingers through his shaggy mane, brushed his face, and put their hands in his mouth. If they so desired they curled down beside him to enjoy together the love of their common Maker. Why not? Some where "the wolf also shall dwell with the lamb and the leopard shall lie down with the kid; and the calf and the young lion and the fatling together; and a little child shall lead them. Their young ones shall lie down together" (Isa. 11 :6-8).

Little children rode the small deer, while older children rode the larger deer or the friendly elephant. All was perfect love. All was great harmony. Such shouts of joy! Such happy childish laughter! Who but our Father in Heaven ever thought of or planned such a Paradise?

Eating and Drinking in the Heaven "Park of Pleasure and Fruits"

When hungry, the children ate of the wonderful fruit or gathered freely the sweet tasting, refreshing manna that was scattered all about. Were they thirsty? Here and there trickled little brooks of the stimulating and refreshing water of life.

Adullam Sees the Bible Saints in Heaven

In the open, lawn-like vistas amidst the trees and flowers and birds of Paradise Adullam saw companies of the redeemed dancing and playing trumpets with the angels.

Sometimes they joined this happy festival group, in which were small children, larger children, and adults, but where no one was old. What heavenly scenes! What heavenly singers! What joy among the angels and the redeemed! The angels pointed out Abraham, David, Daniel, the prophets, the saints, and the martyrs of old. They saw Peter, James, Paul, and others of whom the world was not worthy. Our boy from the poor Miao tribe saw his aunt and his own little sister who had gone ahead to the land "over there." Taking our boys by the hand our little Chinese Mary, who died in Kotchiu, now joined them in heaven.

One Boy Was Given a Vision of The Death of a Christian

As relatives and friends gathered about the dying one an angel stood by the bed, awaiting the liberating of the Christian's soul. When the man was set free from his bodily encumbrance, the angel took him by the arm and ascended with him into heaven. The principalities and powers of evil hosts in mid-heaven in their attempts to hinder the passage of the angel and his charge were overcome by the angel's faith and praise as the ascent continued toward the heavenly city.

Having been welcomed at the gate, this new arrival was received by hosts of angels, singing, dancing, rejoicing, all uniting in giving him a royal welcome into the eternal city of the redeemed.

CHAPTER 6

ANGELS IN OUR MIDST

OUTPOURINGS OF THE HOLY SPIRIT upon Adullam children and young folks have always been attended with visions of angels in our midst.

In this connection it is well to remember some scriptural teaching about angels. The Scriptures teach that angels have a part in the ministration of the Holy Spirit. Since "the spirits (or angels) of the prophets are subject to the prophets" (I Cor. 14:32), angels have some part in prophetic utterance when a prophet speaks under the inspiration of the Holy Spirit. The visions John saw on Patmos and the revelations he had there when he was "in the Spirit" were given him through an angel (Rev. 1:1, 10). Angels therefore have something to do with being in a trance, seeing visions through the Holy Spirit, and getting revelations through the Holy Spirit.

Each true church has, perhaps, a special angel to minister to that particular church (Rev. 1:20). Every saved person has an angel to minister to him (Heb. 1:14, Acts 12 :15) . Every child has the ministry of angels, for the angels of children have constant access to the throne of God in heaven (Matt. 18 :10).32 Angels always see us,33 though we seldom see angels. Angels differ in rank (I Cor. 4 :9) .

Both The Old and New Testament furnish sufficient proof for the reality of angelic ministry in the Adullam Home. We have already told of the visions of angels rescuing children whom demons had bound with awful chains and were dragging to hell. Angels, then, apparently have a part in saving the lost. Since angels led these children to heaven and escorted them through the golden streets and the glories of Paradise, it seems that angels have something to do with the visions given Adullam. As most of the children who spoke in other languages did so when they were dancing and singing with the angels it may be that angels have something to do with speaking in other languages, for it is possible to speak with "the tongues of angels" (I Cor. 13:1) at times of mighty outpourings of the Spirit.

The children also had wonderful visions of multitudes of angels flying in the heavens, and sometimes they saw them fly from heaven to earth.

Angels in the Midst of and about Adullam

At the times when the presence of the Holy Spirit was especially manifest many of the children saw angels near by or in the room. When they were hindered by demon power they saw angels come to their release. On occasions of the most blessed sense of the presence of the Lord in our midst and of the sweetest harmony and love in the meeting, just above the room was a large angel, while the room was entirely surrounded by smaller angels standing side by side, each touching the other to the right and left, so there was not a space in the whole circle for the entrance of any demon. On these occasions, when one or more of the children saw our angel garrison about us, there were never any visions of demons in the room, as was very frequently the case. One evening when our angel guard was about us in such perfect rank children said they could hear demons outside the circle of angels making an angry commotion because of their inability to hinder the blessed fellowship in the Holy Spirit that was within the angels' circle. Boys in Kotchiu had also seen this circle of angels.

I shall never forget the blessed sense of the very presence of God that was in those meetings in which the children saw the angel just above our happy, Spirit-filled people. This angel looking down upon us, smilingly turned from side to side to look at the angels that encircled us and to see that there was not an entrance for the powers of darkness. I wondered if the angel above us was not the special angel of Adullam and if the smaller angels of lesser rank around us were not our individual guardians. At any rate, the children saw the angels. Their eyes were usually closed when they saw them, but sometimes they saw them with wide open eyes. We could believe, without question that we were indeed in the presence of angels.

H.A. BAKER

CHAPTER 7

THE KINGDOM OF THE DEVIL

NO CAREFUL OBSERVER could have been with us during those weeks of the mighty outpouring of the Holy Spirit and doubted that there are two Kingdoms in constant conflict. As surely as angels minister and the Holy Spirit leads to a real Kingdom of light, so surely do demons hinder, while the devil presides in a realm of evil spirits in a kingdom of real darkness. One kingdom was made as certain to us as the other. Man was clearly revealed as the battle ground.

The Bible teaches that there are "the lower ranks of evil spirits and the higher" (Rom. 8:38 Weymouth) and that our conflict is not "with mere flesh and blood but with the despotisms, the empires, the forces that control and govern this dark world" (Eph. 6:12 Weymouth). Both Old and New Testaments teach the reality of a Kingdom of darkness and the reality of demons.

Demons

We related how demons were cast out of one man and how the larger demon was seen to rush about the room in great anger, finally seizing upon an unguarded school teacher, who was looking on, and throwing him to the floor. In this instance two boys saw this big, black, man-like demon enter the man of his possession. Several children saw the cast-out demon, chased out of the room by a Spirit filled young man, take temporary refuge behind some small trees in our court. This demon and the accompanying one about half his size were seen by children who were praying with closed eyes and by some whose eyes were open. But all saw the same things at the same time. The appearance of the demons was the same to each individual.

In the Adullam Rescue Home we had a young girl who very evidently was open to demon activity. She said that before coming here she was subject to "fits," or spells of unconsciousness. A short time after she came she and some of the other girls went for a walk outside the city. On the way back one of the new girls who was half-blind and half-witted lingered behind and lost her way. The older girl, having gone to find the one who was lost, was returning home with her when she saw three demons before her, a few steps away. One was "as tall as a door" and was accompanied by two others about the size of a boy twelve years old. All these demons were dark in appearance, with big eyes and awful faces. The two smaller demons being apparently subject to the large one, obeyed and followed him. The girl was frightened at what she saw. The large demon, coming near, seized her by the head. She became dizzy and almost unconscious. She could scarcely walk. She could hardly see the street and had to be led home by the other girl whom she had gone to seek. Upon reaching home she was better for a time. A little later, while we were at supper, some one came in saying that the afflicted girl was in her room unconscious. We found her prostrate on the floor, breathing as if in a peaceful sleep, but we could not awake her. After praying for her we all assembled in the regular evening prayer meeting. Soon the girl came in perfectly well.

She said that she seemed to be bound by chains and dragged by demons farther and farther down a great dark road, while all the time she was silently praying; then she suddenly realized that the Lord had set her free and she was able to rise. At once she became conscious, and her mind clear. As she sat on her bed alone in the room, she saw the three demons whom she had met on the street now in the room. But now she felt no fear, for she knew that the Lord was Conqueror. Accordingly, she drove the demons out of the room in "the name of Jesus." As they reluctantly receded step by step she followed in the name of Jesus until she drove them along the walk out of the large Chinese door at the entrance of our compound. In the several succeeding months that she was here she had no more "fits" or unconscious spells.

I have given these two instances somewhat in detail, because the effect of demon activity in both cases was so evident that any kind of an observer could have told that something supernatural had taken place. We might tell of many instances of demon activity that have come under our observation the last few years, but these two are sufficient in this connection; we want to tell something of the demon activity in connection with the special outpouring of the Holy Spirit.

When there were manifestations we did not understand we kept praying and trusting the Lord, but decided not to interfere unless we clearly saw something that was harmful or sinful. After eight weeks of wonderful manifestations of the Holy Spirit we were most thankful that we had allowed such liberty among the children. We saw how marvellously the Lord had led them, and things we did not understand at first proved to be part of the Lord's plan in giving us some of the most wonderful and precious revelations.

Among these unusual revelations were those of the...

Demons the Children Saw.

While some of the children were having a blessed time in the Holy Spirit, others went to sleep when they tried to pray. Those under the anointing could often see demons by those who were drowsy and could not pray through. They saw demons coming in through the open window or the door. Sometimes they saw demons lazily reclining under the table or upon a couch that was in the room. Under the anointing of the Holy Spirit, the children, with closed eyes, in the Name of Jesus would rout the demons out of their places and follow them until they went out of the door or window.

They frequently followed these demons out of the room, opened a front or back door to the compound, and chased the demons off the premises. When demons appeared on the scene they were often seen by several persons at the same time.

Some of the children had seen demons before. We found that in spite of all our teaching about the Lord they were still so afraid of demons they dare not go to their rooms alone at night, and they covered their heads when they slept. Through these revelations, however, the children found that the largest and fiercest demons were unavailing against the smallest child covered by Jesus' blood, so that, for the first time, we had a happy lot of Chinese children who had lost their fear of demons, were not afraid in the dark, and were not afraid to sleep with uncovered heads.

You may wonder…

What the Demons were Like.

The demons seen are best described as resembling the demon idols in Chinese temples. According to the Bible and according to the Chinese, much idolatry is demon worship. Making idols of the demon type is an attempt to reproduce the likeness of demons that have been seen.

The children saw demons as "high as a door," with pointed chins and warty heads. There were others of different appearance too, some half this size. There were smaller ones two or three feet high and little ones a few inches high, following the larger demons about.

The large, big-eyed, fierce-looking demons are the ones to be feared as having power to bind and take captives to hell.

The Principalities and Powers of the Air

The hosts of the powers of the air and their works of darkness in co-operation with demons on earth were seen by various Adullam witnesses, whose testimony is as follows:

The government of the hosts of evil is in mid-heaven. Here are thrones from which the devil's angels exercise their Satanic government over the earth. These rulers of darkness vary: some are larger in stature than others; there is variation in dress, crowns, facial expression, disposition, and authority. In all respects they are as devilish in appearance and acts as the hosts of Satan are expected to be.

These rulers of evil are in constant contention among themselves, each resenting the authority of those higher in power, each jealous of the other and all covetous of the seats of highest rank. Those in higher rank hold their positions, not by consent of the lower orders, but solely through their own superior fierceness and power. Cliques and individuals are in constant conflict and quarrels.

All have crowns that represent various orders and ranks. All desire to sit on the thrones above and supervise the work of evil on earth, rather than descend on delegated duties to further the demonical powers below.

Those of highest rank sit on thrones in the mid-heavens, ruling over innumerable hosts of evil spirits, from whose number delegations are constantly dispatched to earth to entice its inhabitants, to withstand the forces of righteousness, to strengthen weak places in the demonical forces of earth, and to bind and to drag the souls of evil men to hell when they die.

Although these wicked angels fly in high heaven to the very gates of the New Jerusalem and although they descend to earth and fly in its air, the center where they congregate in countless numbers is in the region of the thrones of authority in the mid-heavens. Here evil hosts of wicked spirits of all sizes fly hither and thither or move about more deliberately. A certain halo surrounds the wicked angels of higher rank.

All are similar in some respects: All have wings, all have crowns, all belong in the heavens. The delegated messengers go to earth only temporarily. Their evil errand finished, they again return to the heavens.

The hosts of **evil spirits on earth** are very different from the devil's **angels**. These on earth do not have wings; they can walk and run rapidly; and they move freely but apparently do not leave the earth. They vary in size from a few inches to ten feet in height, wear gaudy colored clothes of many stripes, and have fancy caps of various shapes and colors; some, on the other hand, wear rags or filthy garments.

Some of these demons on earth have very little power and are of a rather harmless order. Others, however, are large in stature, fierce in appearance, and have great power. These on earth withstand the work of righteous men and the work of angels among men. In one of their conflicts with an angel, earthly demons of highest rank, assisted by others of lower rank, gathered about the angel, trying to strike him with clubs, swords, and other weapons. Through faith and praising the Lord, the angel so with stood this onslaught that no blow fell upon him nor could an evil hand touch him. The demons of less power, standing at a little distance and watching the conflict, upon seeing their companions unsuccessful in their attack, besought the powers of evil in the heavens to send a re-enforcement of the devil's angels from the air. In response to this entreaty a detachment of ten angels were sent down. As these approached the earth the demons below clapped their hands in joyous welcome. When the wicked angels from above reached the scene of conflict these less powerful demons, receding a distance, stood in respectful quietness in the presence of the Satanic delegation from above, who now took up the conflict with the angel. These forces the angel also withstood with praises and faith until suddenly the Glory of God descended and entirely routed all the hosts of evil.

The boy who saw a Christian die also saw...

What Takes Place When the Unconverted Die.

When one man who did not know the Gospel died, his soul, after being liberated from the body, wandered about unhindered from place to place on earth, until one of the devil's angels, descending from the sky with chains, bound him and forced him down to hell. The death of a professing Christian who had known the Lord, but had not truly repented, was still more terrible. When this man was dying, demons by his deathbed waited in fiendish delight for the liberation of the soul of this hypocritical, one-time professing Christian. The demons began to bind him before he was entirely out of the body and completed the binding of their captive the minute he drew his last ungodly breath. The hypocrite did not enjoy one moment of freedom to wander about the earth. An object of ridicule to his demon captors, in terror he was at once dragged and pushed into hell.

One such ungodly man was the special sport of demons who, having bound him in chains, dragged him along on the earth, again and again jerking him up on his feet only again to drag him down and haul him along like a dead dog. After furnishing amusement for his captor the man was dragged down the dark road to the infernal regions.

There was...

A Boy Dragged from Adullam to Hell

because he had been so bad he was discharged as errand boy by an officer in the army. After seeing him begging on the street for several days we took him into the Adullam Rescue Home. He promised to reform, made an outward showing of decency, heard the Gospel for a considerable time, and professed repentance.

Different articles disappeared from the Home, but the thief was not found until this boy was caught on his way to sell the stolen plunder. We then put him out of the Home.

After several months of beggar life, during which time this boy repeatedly promised to reform if only we would allow him to return, we gave him another chance. The Lord also gave him another chance, for there were manifestations of the Holy Spirit and supernatural revelations sufficient to make the way of life clear to the most simple. This boy himself had anointings of the Holy Spirit, when the Lord dealt directly with him about his sins and showed him the better way. In spite of all this the boy ran away and joined a street gang of beggar-thieves. A few months later he fell and broke his arm, infection set in, and he was about to die when he was picked up by a hospital worker. In the hospital he was so hopelessly disobedient that he was thrown out and was soon in a dying condition on the street. Coming to us with promises of repentance, we pitied him and took him in once more.

Day by day he neared the end of the way. The night before he died I was awakened by unearthly shrieks that sounded like uncanny howls of some wild animal or of some fiend. The next day when the boy died I was away from home. As he lay in death throes, delighted, awful hellish demons gathered about him. When his soul was leaving his body the boy seeing his captors, wept, yelled, shrieked, and cried at the top of his voice in wildest terror; "Mr. Baker, help! help! help! O, Mr. Baker, come quickly! Mr. Baker, Mr. Baker, Mr. Baker! Help, they are all about me with chains! They have come for me. Help, help, Mr. Baker, help! Oh, oh, oh, help! help! help! They are binding me with chains. Help! help! Oh, oh, oh, help! Oh h—e—l—p"

Visions of Hell

Over and over again children had visions of hell and the lake of fire. The first time any one was under the anointing of the Spirit he usually had a vision of hell. He was bound in chains by demons and taken through a region of darkness. Some children could hear demons all about them in this region. If taken far, they could see a dim light in the distance which proved to be reflections from the lake of fire. Some children were forced so near they could see the lake of fire ahead. All the time they were pleading the blood of Christ, asserting that they would not obey and would not be subject to the slavery of their captors. They believed Jesus would surely save. We have already told how at this climax, before the lake of fire was reached, the Lord did intervene with His blood-bought salvation.

The Bible pictures hell as a place of blackness and darkness,35 and it teaches that part of the devil's angels are now reserved in chains of darkness awaiting judgment.

The children saw not only darkness in hell, but also…

The Lake of Fire

that was always approached through a region of stygian darkness.36 In vision they were led to the edge of a great lake of molten fire in a semi-dark pit from which arose clouds of smoke. When the smoke settled low the fire in the lake was less distinct. When the smoke lifted a little, the burning lake with red and greenish flames and its inmates could be distinctly seen.

When the children were peering down into this pit in hell we saw them taking a firm hold on some piece of furniture or getting down on their hands and knees, cautiously bending forward to peep into the infernal regions. They looked a moment and then drew back, afraid lest they fall in. They were horrified at what they saw. Then very cautiously they looked again and drew back. Sometimes the children lay flat on their stomachs, lest they slip and fall while looking over the brink of the lake of fire.

The lost were seen going into hell. Some fell in, some walked over the brink, and some were bound by demon chains and cast into hell by demons. One boy saw groups of the wicked bound in bundles, ready to be cast into this furnace of fire.37

When the fire abated and the smoke settled down the moans of the miserable could be heard. When the fire at intervals increased in intensity and the smoke lifted a little there were shrieks and wails of agony.

One person was rolled on the floor and caused to cry out as would a suffering soul in hell.

In the lake of fire were oceans of hands reaching up for help. Those below appealed to those looking in upon them to come to their rescue. We could hear the children talking to them just as you can hear some one talking over the telephone and get but one end of the conversation. We could hear one end of a conversation like this: "I can't help you." "No, I cannot do anything for you." "But when you were alive you would not obey the gospel." "No, it is too late; before you got here I preached to you, but you made fun of me and despised Jesus. Now you know I told you the truth." "No, I cannot do anything; this is the judgment of God." "If you had obeyed, you would now be enjoying heaven with us." After some such conversation the children were led away to enjoy the presence of Jesus in heaven or the glories of the golden streets of the Paradise of God.

Lazarus could see the rich man in hell tormented in flames, and the rich man could talk with Lazarus, but he could not cross the gulf. When Christ reigns as King of Kings upon the earth the redeemed nations will look upon the lost.38

One boy saw his grandmother in hell, whom he had tried to win to Christ. She was once a sorceress and murderer who had withstood the gospel she heard in her village and caused many to refuse the light. Other children also had visions of relatives in hell. This tribal boy who saw his grandmother in hell was the boy who saw his little sister and his believing aunt in heaven.

There was no vision of any one in heaven or the name of any one on the mansions by the golden streets who did not trust in Jesus. Those in hell were all unbelievers. One night when the Lord spoke through a small boy in wonderful prophecy, among the things he said was, "There will be no one in heaven except those who believe the gospel."

After the Lord had taken the boys and girls through most wonderful and systematic lessons in the Holy Spirit they nearly all came at last to...

The Parting of the Roads.

In this vision, repeated until it seemed the impression could never be forgotten, the one in vision seemed to be standing by the cross at the parting of the two great roads. The one was the narrow way of life that leads to heaven and glory; the other was the broad way to hell and destruction.

Great, busy, hurrying multitudes—multitudes hustling with business, carrying great loads of sin and rushing along with the affairs of life—were passing by in endless streams and countless numbers. The child was the preacher at the cross roads. Again we heard one side of the conversation: "Hello! my friend! Please wait a minute; I want to speak to you. Say, do not go down that broad road; it leads to hell and ruin. I have been down that way and have seen hell for myself. Stop here by the cross and let Jesus wash all your sins away. From the Cross of Christ here you can start up this other road that will lead you to heaven and everlasting life and joy. Oh! that fellow does not believe it. There he goes on down the broad road. What a pity! I will stop this other man and see if he will believe. Hey there! Just a minute! Say, do not follow that crowd. They do not know where they are going. That road leads to destruction; that is the road to the lake of fire. Please don't go on. I came out here to stop as many of you as possible and give you fair warning. Better turn aside here, let Jesus wash your sins away, and go with us up the road to heaven where God is. Oh, there he goes, too!

"Here is another. Wait a moment! Say, come out of that crowd. Cannot you see there is no one traveling back this way? They all go down that road; no one ever comes back. That is the broad road to hell. Stop here by the cross, believe the gospel of salvation through Jesus' blood, and you will be safe. There is no other road further on. This is the only road to heaven. Turn in here or you will be lost too.

"Oh, what a pity he does not believe me. There he goes with the others."

Sometimes the youthful preacher would decide that if no one believed him he would follow the wilful crowd to see what happened. When he arrived with the crowd at the brink of the lake of fire in hell, we heard him say, "Look at that crowd falling into hell! Not one escapes. Everyone goes in." Slowly drawing near the edge of the pit and leaning over and looking down into the lake with its suffering multitudes, the preacher said: "I can not help you now. I told you all about this back there at 'the gospel cross roads,' but you would not believe. No, you would not believe, even if I could help you out. No, I am helpless now. If you had listened when I warned, the Lord would have saved you; you came on and fell in because you would not take advice. No, I can't. I am going back to the cross roads to see if I can find some one who will listen, and stop a few at any cost."

He was occasionally successful in persuading one to listen. Then he would say, "Now, you get down there at the foot of the cross of Jesus and pray. Oh, you don't know how to pray? Well, you say what I tell you. 'Jesus, I am a sinner! I was on my road to hell. I am only fit for hell. The big load I carry is only sin. Forgive my sins and teach me to live only for your glory. Amen'" There was rejoicing then as the sinner was saved and started up the narrow road, while the preacher went out to try to rescue another deluded traveler.

These visions, with some variations, were repeated many times, making it clear that salvation was only by repentance and belief in the blood of Christ, through the preaching of the gospel; that the many were called; that few were saved; that the road to destruction is broad and multitudes pass that way; that the way of life is narrow and few there be that find it.39 It was made equally clear that the Christian is to stand in the gap at the parting of the ways and persuade and warn to the limit of his ability.

We have told how the boys, even the small boys, went out at that time and preached on the streets with unction of the Holy Spirit, sometimes under direct inspiration such as we had never before witnessed. I will close this chapter with the story of...

The University Student Who Went by the Cross Roads.

Opposite our front gate lived a university student who was to have graduated from the university that year. After moving here I talked with him, asking him to come over and discuss the Bible and Christianity in a friendly way. He came a few days, and I felt certain he was convinced of the truth of what I said. The questions he raised seemed to be answered to his full satisfaction.

Through him I managed to get a chance to talk with some of the other university students during their vacation. I had been going to their rooms ten days, when there came the mighty outpouring of the Holy Spirit upon Adullam. The students were friendly, and I felt that the student I have mentioned saw clearly the truth of the gospel. I could see that, although he was polite, he was not disposed to accept the truth and did not seem to like the friendly way the other students responded to the Bible discussions.

One morning when one of our girls was out at our front gate it happened that this young university student was out there too.

The girl began telling him he ought to be a Christian, in a simple way urging him to believe in Jesus to save him from his sins, make him a good man, save him from hell, and lead him to heaven.

"What's the use of my being a Christian? I do not need to be saved."

"You might die suddenly in your sins, and you would go to hell."

"Who are you?" scoffed the student. "You are a little snip of an ignorant girl, just a sort of useless beggar. What do you suppose you are trying to do? You are trying to teach me something when you are not worthy to even talk to me. I am a university student. I am wise. I have read many books. I have been many years in Peking. I can speak and read English as well as Chinese." He then spat in her face and told her to mind her own business.

Two weeks later hearing a funeral commotion in the front alley, I was surprised to learn that they were carrying this university student to his burial; I had seen him on the street a few days before. One of the boys said that as we were going out to preach, a few days previous, he had offered this young man a tract, but he would not take it.

I knew nothing of this conversation with the girl. About a month later this girl was in a trance under the power of the Spirit. After seeing visions of heaven and the glories of the redeemed she stood still and bent over as though looking into hell. This is what I heard: "Ah! There is hell. No, I cannot; I have no power to help you now. You certainly are in an awful plight. It is you who are worse than a beggar now, all dirty, all filthy, and suffering in the lake of fire. In fact, you look worse now than any beggar I ever saw. I thought you told me you were rich and that you had a great education. Where is your education now? Well, I cannot help you now even if you do apologize. That may be, but I have no power. No, only Jesus can save you, but when I told you about Him you made fun of Him and cursed me.

"Look what we beggars who believe in Jesus have received in heaven: all is joy, all is happiness; all is love in the city of golden streets with its wonderful Paradise of God."

The Righteous Scarcely Saved

Then the girl seemed to be crossing the lake of fire over a narrow bridge. We saw her walking as though she were walking a rope, placing one foot carefully in front of the other while extending her arm on either side until she recovered her balance. With a sigh of relief she said, "My! This is dangerous! But the Lord will help me. I will get across to the other side." Then she carefully brought the other foot forward and nearly lost her balance again. She praised the Lord until she recovered her balance and proceeded as before. In this way having crossed the room, she seemed to be safely in heaven, past every danger of ever falling into the lake of fire.

Whatever the effect of relating these visions may have on others, these things have taught us in Adullam to believe more assuredly than ever in the reality of heaven and the Kingdom of God and the reality of hell and the Kingdom of the devil. More positively than ever do we assert that the way through this life that leads over the dangers of the lake of fire, the way that "over-comers" must travel, is like walking a rope which must be traveled step by step with fear and trembling.40 Only the Lord Jesus can sustain us in the balance so that we may not topple in to the right, or escaping that, fall to the left. We are surer than ever that God means for us to stand by the cross at the cross roads to point sinners to the narrow, little-traveled road that starts at the cross and leads by it on up to heaven and the life the Lord has prepared for them who love Him. How can any be saved without this salvation; how can any escape who neglect this salvation? "For if the word spoken through angels proved steadfast, and every transgression and disobedience received a just recompense of reward; how shall we escape, if we neglect so great a salvation" (Heb. 2 :2, 3)?

CHAPTER 8

END OF THIS AGE AND THE RETURN OF CHRIST

DURING THE MIGHTY OUT POURING of the Holy Spirit, by vision and prophecy we were repeatedly warned that the end of the present age and the return of our Lord is at hand.

The Holy Spirit made this great climax at the consummation of the present age so vivid and real that no doubt was left in any of our minds that the Lord God was bringing last and supremely important messages to his people.

The Scripture teaches that the present age will end in the greatest tribulation the world has ever seen and that immediately after that tribulation the Lord will return to destroy the wicked and reward the righteous.[41]

The Scriptures also teach that this age will reach its climax at its "end" in the harvest when the tares will have reached full fruition and when the wheat will have passed from the leaf and the blade to the full grain in the ear. When both the wheat and the tares are ripe the angels will come with the Lord to gather the harvest and to separate the wheat from the tares. In other words, when the Kingdom of the devil is at its worst and the

Kingdom of God on earth is at its best, in its purest form the evil ripe and the good ripe—then will come the harvest.42 The Bible further teaches that evil will reach its climax in the incarnation of the devil in control of a demon-deceived and tormented world and that this devil-possessed world ruler, the super-man, will be destroyed by the Lord at his coming.43

There may be those who take exception to the above remarks, but, without detailed discussion of these matters, I will relate, as best I can, the visions and revelations given Adullam children, who knew little or nothing of the theology involved.

Pestilence and Wars

Time after time they spoke in prophecy, saying that a time of famine, pestilence, war, and desolation is coming and that it will be attended with persecution of the people of God, whom He will especially equip and protect in this crisis.

One boy saw our school teacher trying to buy a measure of rice. So great a crowd surrounded the granary that the teacher could only hope for success in making his purchase by pushing with the crowd. Only one measure of rice could be bought by each man.44

In vision one ignorant, uneducated boy was transported to our civilized lands and saw the peoples getting ready for war, making bombs, cannon, and implements of destruction.

The coming of the devil and his incarnation in the Antichrist was prophesied many times, as well as seen in vision.

Visions of the Devil and Antichrist

The children saw the dragon, the devil with seven heads. One boy saw angels fighting with him and seven of his angels. The devil and his angels were overcome and flung out of heaven to earth.45

Adullam boys saw the super-man the world is wishing for, the great subject of worship that Buddhism, Theosophy, Mohammedanism and other religions expect. In him they saw the devil incarnated as a handsome, strong man in the beauty and strength of young manhood.

They also had visions of the image that in due season this God-defying Antichrist will erect according to prophecy as an object of worship, the image that will be able to speak and to deceive the world.46 I asked how they knew this handsome man of power was the Antichrist. They said that a host of demons followed him everywhere, obeyed his every command, advanced at his word, and halted at his order.

This Antichrist was also seen upon a plain as a beast with seven heads. Again I asked how they knew this was the Antichrist, and the children said the angels told them. I have already explained that, as to John, these revelations were given through angels when the children were "in the Spirit" in a trance and that, like him, they carried on conversation with the angels and by these heavenly messengers were told the mystery of many things they did not understand themselves.

The Saints Under Persecution

During the reign of this super-man in his God-defying power the saints of God were standing true and bearing faithful testimony in spite of every hardship and every danger. They saw the two witnesses in Jerusalem, and they saw the saints, as well as these two, endued with mighty supernatural power to fight with and to resist the power of darkness in that awful time, the like of which has never been upon the earth—the time when the devil and all his angels and demons will be turned loose upon the earth, having great wrath, knowing their time is short. During this time, when no one but a true Spirit-filled saint could stand for a day against such Satanic power and supernatural Satanic miracles and manifestations, the children saw the saints filled with the still greater supernatural power of their God, the Spirit of him, who is greater than "he that is in the world." They had visions of preaching the gospel in the midst of great persecution; but they were given such power that by a word from them, enemies smitten by plagues47 or death. This power seemed to issue from within and came out of their mouths; with it they rebuked and slew their enemies. They were exercising the power the Lord had promised his disciples, power to do the works He did and greater works.48 In some cases, after giving a testimony in a town that rejected them and having left it a distance, fire from heaven descended and destroyed the wicked place, even as Sodom and Gommorah were swept away. When persecution was bitter they were some times caught away bodily by the Holy Spirit as was Philip49 and as the prophets supposed Elijah had been (II Kings 2:16). They were thus by the Spirit carried away to a place of safety. In time of hunger and need food was miraculously provided—manna, fruit, and other food. Angels ministered. Strength and boldness were given to bear a fearless testimony. The Christians had power to speak with tongues in the languages of strange and unevangelized tribes. When in vision the boys or girls were thus preaching in the Spirit we ourselves could see how this might be true, for while one speaker preached to the people of a strange language whom he saw before him, another interpreted for him (I Cor. 14:28). Both spoke in other tongues. One spoke a few sentences, then the other interpreted. They were preaching to some of those of every tribe and language.

John saw an angel flying in heaven with the everlasting gospel to be preached to all tribes and tongues, just before the fall of Babylon the Great.50 He also saw a great multitude no man could number, people of every tribe and language, who had washed their robes in the blood of the Lamb and had come out of Great Tribulation.51 Must it not be in accord with the Scripture that, as the children saw in these visions, the gospel will be preached again under angelic ministration in the miraculous power of the Holy Spirit in a supernatural way, far exceeding that of the early Church in the days of its persecution? May it not be that the harvest outpouring of the Holy Spirit, the latter rain, will far exceed the seed-time outpouring of the Holy Spirit, the former rain, the outpouring on the Day of Pentecost?

The Final World War

At the conclusion of the final testimony of the most perfect and supernatural church the world has ever seen, in the midst of the greatest persecution by the greatest concentration of Satanic demonical power and devil-controlled human power that any age on earth has ever experienced, the Adullam children saw the Antichrist, the devil-man, the super-man world leader, marshalling his forces for the final world war of the age.

They also saw the war in the spirit realm. In this they saw a man on a white horse, leading his army of angels dressed in white.52 They also saw a rider on a red horse, the rider dressed in beautiful dark colored array and followed by his host of demons in black.

Some visions of the war on earth were also seen. Children saw battleships destroyed by bombs thrown from airplanes, and they saw the ships with all aboard enter their watery grave to be seen no more. Armies were seen gathered from all the earth, engaged in the great and terrible struggle. The children watched the awful battle. Poison gas and deadly instruments of war slew their victims in countless numbers. At first the dead were buried, but later the slain, being so many they could not be taken care of, were piled in heaps or left to decay as manure upon the face of the earth, as the prophet has foretold.53 In the midst of all these things everything was interrupted by...

The Sudden Return of Christ.

The sun became dark and the moon red like blood.54 The stars fell in showers. The heavens shook and seemed to roll together as a scroll. There was a great earthquake that rent the earth asunder. Great crevices opened and people were swallowed alive. Buildings were shaken down, collapsing like children's toy houses, killing and burying the inmates. While these things in heaven and earth were taking place the Lord appeared in the heavens. Old and young, rich and poor were overcome with deadly fear. They fled in every direction in wild confusion. Men fled from their shops empty handed, without a thought of their valuables that a few moments before had seemed of great importance. Families rushed from their homes without even a glance back upon the luxuries that had been their life passion. In one moment all men became one in purpose; they had only one desire; they sought only one thing. That one desire was to flee from the face of the returning Judge; they sought only a place of refuge to hide from the visible King of Kings. Some who were not killed by falling houses or who did not tumble into the opened earth tried to flee to the mountains for safety; some leaped into the rivers and perished; some slew themselves with their own weapons.

Everywhere was wailing and shrieking. Everywhere was riot and terror. Anything to escape from the wrath of the Lamb, for the great day of His wrath was come.

After this there were visions of…

The Great Supper of God,

where the beasts and birds were bidden to eat the unburied dead that lay scattered over the ruined earth. Dogs and wild animals were seen feeding on the carcasses of men. Birds and scavengers of the air joined in this supper prepared by God.

While the boys were witnessing this great feast we could hear their remarks and see their movements as the scene was described and acted out before us. One would say, "Look at that eagle eating that rich fellow. See it picking his fancy clothes from his body. Look at that! It has taken a piece of his flesh and flown away."

Another said, "O, look over there; a vulture and a crow both eating at that man. The vulture has the most courage. He just picks and picks away, gorging himself, never taking time to look up, but the crow is afraid; he takes a bit and looks around to see if he is in danger. 'Ai ya,' do you see that? Look at the birds standing on that well dressed fellow and digging into him." Then the boys suddenly with one accord wheeled around with their backs toward the repellent scene, while their remarks, as well as their motions, made it clear enough the sort of abhoring scenes that will characterize the final feast of the earth. Here will be the rich and mighty, the captains of the earth, the captains of industry, the captains of wealth, the captains of war, and the captains of all Christ-rejecting enterprises and religions. They will not be there as honored guests, but as the food for the scavengers of the earth over which they have lived in selfish luxury.

Thus the Adullam children have already seen and described in terrible reality the culminating scenes of our boasted material civilization. They have seen the fruit of godless sowing and the answer to the question of our Lord, "What shall it profit a man if he gain the whole world and lose his own soul?" The Word of God says, "All the nations that forget God shall be turned into hell." These simple children believe without a doubt, because they have been shown by God and the angels what is also written in the Word of the Lord, that the climax and consummation of the present world with its human systems of education and its boasted organization and wealth will be "the great supper of God," where the flesh of the dead will be more of a prize than will be the splendor and culture that is now the pride of the living.

The Antichrist Bound and the Devil Cast into the Pit

The children saw the Lord and his angels bind the Antichrist hand and foot, preparatory to casting him alive into hell.[56]

There were visions also of the devil taken alive to the mouth of the pit; a box-like lid was lifted up, and he was cast down into the black well-like shaft of the abyss; the lid was shut down, and the Lord locked it with a great key.[57]

The Descent of the Lord and the Last Trumpet

We have written of the visions of the return of Christ as related to the wicked. There were equally clear visions relating to the saints. Adullam saw the heavens open and the Lord descend in glory attended by His angels. On either side and following the Lord was this great army of attendants in white. Those in front blew beautiful trumpets as with the blast of trumpets the Lord and His army descended in perfect order, every one keeping in his proper place and rank. As the Lord thus descended toward the earth there were wonderful visions of the...

Resurrection and Rapture of the Saints.

Graves burst open as from an explosion. Bodies came out of the graves and were suddenly clothed upon by the heavenly tabernacle of the resurrection glory life. In some cases bones were seen to come together as the children expressed it in Chinese idiom: "one bone from the east and one from the west." These scattered bones, having become clothed with flesh and transformed into the resurrection body, were caught up to meet the Lord in the air.[58] One boy saw a funeral procession where a Christian was being carried to his burial. On the way to the burial ground the trumpet sounded, the Lord descended, the coffin opened, the dead sat up, arose transformed, and ascended into the air.

I have already told how our children had visions of some of our Adullam people already dead and now in heaven, clothed in white and enjoying Paradise and of their seeing the saints of old clothed in white. The Scripture teaches that between death and the resurrection the saints have spiritual bodies and that the saints are clothed in white **before** the time of the resurrection.59 When I cross-questioned the children as to how they knew whether the saints they saw in heaven had been resurrected or not, they said they did not know until the angels told them that they saw only the souls of the saints and that their bodies had not been resurrected. I questioned and cross-questioned in some of these matters and always got a uniform testimony: the children always saw the saints in white; the saints never had wings; all of the angels had wings; there was no difficulty in distinguishing between saints and angels.

In summary, then, Adullam saw the saints in white now in heaven, with access to Paradise, and enjoying the fellowship of Christ and the angels; they saw the descent of the Lord with "all his holy ones"—all his angels—at the sounding of the last trumpet; they saw the resurrection and transformation of the bodies of the saints and their ascent into the air. They also saw…

The Marriage Supper of the Lamb.

Great tables were spread in Paradise in the midst of its magnificent trees, its wonderful flowers with enchanting fragrance, its glorious birds of every plumage that sang their carols of praise, where all redeemed animal and vegetable creation was one harmonious, spirit-filled, God-praising whole. Here, then, in this indescribable Paradise of God in open spaces were spread the tables for the great Marriage Supper. Angels and the glorified saints skipped about everywhere playing harps, blowing trumpets, singing, and praising the Lord. Some of the children acted out these scenes before us. They hurried to their jewel bedecked home to get their harp or trumpet and joined the spirit inspired music of the greatest of all festival scenes, the climax of all the hopes of the ages. Great companies sang, and danced, and praised the King. Others hurried about preparing the tables or the seats and carrying the golden dishes of food.

There was abundance of food, everything having flavor of its own, exceeding anything that could be imagined.

When all was ready, the call was sent forth and the saints of all past ages gathered around the tables to celebrate the wedding of the King's Great Son. The consummation of all their hopes, the realization of all highest joy in heaven itself, came to its highest point when the harlot, the beggar, the sinner, and the one-time off-scourings of the earth came from the east and the west and sat down with Abraham, Isaac, and Jacob at this festal table in the Kingdom of God.[61] As all arose and expectantly reached its greatest height, the Son Himself came in and sat down at the tables surrounded by his blood bought and white-robe clad bride the redeemed of every nation, and tribe, and tongue and drank with them the fruit of the vine.[62]

Adullam saw…

The Books Opened and the Day of Judgment.

They saw the books in which the deeds of men are recorded and saw the Judge upon the throne before whom all men were judged out of the books. The righteous were set apart to stand in one great company on the one side, while those whose names were not in the book of life were gathered into another great company to stand on the other side. The one company was separated to enter the Kingdom of God and the life of the ages; the other group was doomed to go into the fire prepared for the devil and his angels.[63]

A few were privileged to have visions of…

The New Heaven and the New Earth.

The New Heaven was so filled with Shekina glory that the children could not carefully look into it.

The New Jerusalem, the city four-square, occupied the central position in the New Earth. They saw the celestial city with its Paradise as it is now, but descended upon the New Earth. The whole New Earth was much like the Paradise that is now and will then still be in the city of God, the Bride of the Lamb.64 It was the earth God wanted for His children, more than restored by Him who is more than Conqueror. It was the New Heaven and the New Earth that had passed through the new birth65 and that will never pass away, the earth where God will again pitch his tent with men, where he will forever be called their God and they shall all and always be His Children. Amen.

H.A. BAKER

CHAPTER 9

CHINESE BEGGER BOY PROPHECIES

IN FULFILMENT OF THE SCRIPTURE that "in the last days. .. your sons . . . shall prophesy" (Acts 2 :17), one of the little ten-year-old beggar sons of China was used as the mouthpiece of the Lord to bring us a message by **direct inspiration**.

A few months previous this boy, ragged and dirty—in fact, more nearly clothed with filth than with garments—came to our door with his two companions to ask if he might come in. When bathed and dressed, the boy looked like a guileless little fellow, and such he proved to be. He at once took every Bible story and sermon to heart. He soon learned to pray, and we could hear him praying in bed very earnestly every night. When the Holy Spirit fell upon us this boy was among the first to receive the baptism of the Spirit, speaking with other tongues as on the Day of Pentecost.

As surely as ever God spoke in the past, when men were moved upon by the Holy Spirit, so that Scripture was inspired of God and prophets declared their message to be "Thus saith the Lord" with such assurance that they were ready to back their convictions with their lives, even so surely the living God still reigns and speaks to the children of men by direct prophecy, when the circumstances demand it, and faith and other conditions are according to His divine will.

One night the power of the Lord was present in an unusual manner. Heaven seemed not far away. Then it was that our one-time, little, friendless beggar-boy seemed to leave this filthy earth and to be caught up to heaven. Ushered into the presence of the Lord Jesus, he fell prostrate at His feet in humble adoration and worship. As a matter-of-fact, the boy lay prostrate in the middle of the room surrounded by his companions, who sat about him on the floor, listening intently to a message that came through him from the Lord. Such gripping, heart-searching words I have never heard. While the boy sobbed and wept with deepest grief the message was given, a sentence or two at a time, in a clear strong voice. The language came in rhythm; the choice of words was the simplest and purest. The intonation of the voice, the choice of language, the penetrating power of every word was such that no person who heard could ever doubt that this little simple minded Samuel was speaking by direct supernatural inspiration from God.

Prostrated in vision at the feet of the Lord, the boy said, "Lord Jesus, I am not worthy to be here or to be saved at all. I am only a little street beggar." Then Jesus addressed the boy. The boy did not know it at the time, but the Lord actually spoke **through** the boy as a mouth piece, using the first person and addressing us and the children sitting about him. Here is the "Thus saith the Lord" that we wish might grip your hearts as it still grips our own.

The Message from Christ

"I weep tonight. I am heart-broken. I am in deep sorrow because those who believe in me are so very few. I planned and prepared heaven for every one, having made room for all the people in all the world. I made the New Jerusalem in three great cities, one above the other, with plenty of space for all men. But men will not believe me. Those who believe are so very few. I am sad, so very sad. (This message was given between heart-rending sobs and floods of tears from the boy.) Since men will not believe me, I must destroy the wicked earth. I planned to visit it with three great calamities, but it is so wicked that I have added a fourth.

"If you have any friends, tell them to repent quickly; persuade all men as rapidly as possible to believe the gospel; but if people will not listen and will not accept your message the responsibility will not be upon you.

"Get the baptism of the Holy Spirit. If you will tarry and believe, I will baptize you. The devil deceives you by making you think you will not receive the baptism, but wait and seek and I will baptize you, and give you power to cast out devils and to heal the sick. Those who receive the seal of the Holy Spirit are to preach and testify, and I will be with you to help and protect you in times of danger.

"If you think perhaps you will not get to heaven, that thought is of the devil. I will not destroy my own children; I will protect and save every one; not one of mine will perish. I will overcome. Pray for Mr. and Mrs. Baker and I will give them power to cast out devils and to heal the sick. The children in the home should obey. Do not fight. Do not lie. Live at peace. When you pray, pray from the heart. Do not let your love grow cold.

"Tell other churches they, too, should seek the Holy Spirit. All churches must press forward.

"The devil is coming to earth in a few years, and there will be great tribulation. Do not worry; I will protect and care for you.

"People everywhere will gather together and fight in one place, after which I will come to punish the earth. You must not fear, for those who believe in me will be caught up to blow trumpets and to play harps.

"I will destroy two of every three. When I come everything

must obey my voice (Chinese, "Yang yang du yao ting o dy hwa"). Houses will tumble down; mountains will fall; trees will be destroyed. There will be utter destruction where I will not leave one blade of grass (Chinese, "Ih gen tsao du buh liu"). Those who worship idols will perish. All sorcerers and spiritist mediums shall be cast into hell. Only those who believe the gospel will be saved."

Thus hath the Lord spoken to Adullam and, we believe, to all to whom we may be able to pass this message of prophecy. This message from our risen Lord was given in Chinese as above recorded, the sentences spoken slowly and distinctly with pauses between. I wrote them as they were given, often repeated a time or two so there could be no mistake on the part of the hearers; there was ample time to record without mistake every word the Lord spoke through this little inspired prophet of His choice.

The message complete, the little boy arose and told us he had been at the feet of Jesus. He did not know that the Lord had spoken **through** him as well as **to** him in the first person. He repeated the prophecy, saying, "Jesus said that, Jesus said this," etc.

This prophecy already heard, already written, and then again repeated from the little prophet's memory item by item, made it easy to see how in days of old the prophets spoke as moved by God, how a scribe might record every word as it came from the lips of the prophet, or how the prophet himself could record his own messages, truly saying, "thus saith the Lord."

In days of old, when religious and worldly men had departed from a simple faith in a personal living God who spoke to men and when their unbelief and wickedness was such that "in those days there was no open vision" (I Sam 3), God found a pure-minded little Samuel and spoke to him in an **audible voice** a message that was fulfilled to the very letter. Accordingly, we believe that God who is still the same **living God** that has spoken to and through others in the **past** has, in this day of wickedness and unbelief, given to us through our little Chinese Samuel a "Thus saith the Lord" that will shortly come to pass, a message to be heeded to our eternal joy or neglected to eternal sorrow.

CHAPTER 10

SOME LIGHT ON WRITING THE BIBLE

THROUGH THIS OUTPOURING of the Holy Spirit upon these Chinese children much light was thrown upon the writing of the Word of God.

Prophecy Fulfilled

Such an outpouring of the Spirit, attended with such supernatural manifestations, is in itself a testimony that the Bible was written by God. He alone knows the future. **Fulfilled prophecy** was, in the mind of Christ and the apostles, sufficient proof of the hand of God in the writing of the Scriptures.

In what we have recorded about this outpouring of the Holy Spirit upon these children ten prophecies of the Scriptures were fulfilled: (1) such a baptism was prophesied for believers of the present age; (2) it was to be accompanied by speaking in unknown languages and by (3) prophesying as the Spirit gave utterance. (4) In fulfilment of prophecy these children were shown "the things of Christ." (5) The reality of "things to come" was also shown them. (6) True to prophecy, they were "born again" of the Holy Spirit, receiving the witness in their hearts crying, "Abba Father." (7) The visions seen by these children fulfilled the written Word that in the last days "young men shall see visions." (8) Demons were cast out, and (9) the sick were miraculously healed, just as the Bible said they might be, by the power of the Holy Spirit. (10) A miraculous change took place so that things once loved were hated and things once hated were loved.

The Ignorant Confound the Wise

It is to be recalled that, according to the Bible, the revelations of God and the writings of the Scriptures are independent of natural ability or of acquired education. An uneducated Amos, or Peter, or John, inspired by God, wrote more profoundly than the wisest of this world.

In what the Lord has done and revealed to these despised and outcast beggar boys and girls can we not see a proof of the Word of God? While "not many wise after the flesh, not many mighty" follow the old-fashioned, narrow way of simple faith in God, He still can and does choose these "that are despised," even these simple Chinese children of the streets and gutters, to "bring to naught the things that are" supposed to be so learned and wise, in this age of godless reason and worldly knowledge.

While the wise of this learned, proud, and stiff necked generation that resists the simple Word go on groping around in the darkness of their own self-sufficient delusions, it must be true in this day, as in the past, that in the midst of so much confusion of man's wisdom, Jesus can still say, "I thank Thee, O Father, Lord of heaven and earth, that Thou didst hide these things from the wise and understanding, and didst reveal them unto babes" (Matt. 11 :25).

As a whole, the educated and the rulers of the days of Christ did not understand His miraculous works and life, or "they would not have crucified the Lord of Glory" (I Cor. 2:8). The rulers and the educated of the days of the apostles did not understand the miraculous working of Almighty God through simple men endued with the power of the Holy Spirit, or they would not have killed the Spirit-filled saints of the early Church. The profound revelations to these Chinese children "not having learned" in the schools of worldly letters is a corroboration of the written word of God that it came, as it claims to have come, through open hearted men independent of natural ability or acquired education.

Eye Witnesses of Past Bible Events

Some clear light was thrown on the way Bible writers might have had an eye-witness knowledge of events already past. One of our naturally most ignorant and untalented boys was, on more than one occasion when "in the Spirit," an eye witness of the principal historical events of the Old and New Testaments. He saw the plagues of Egypt: the frogs in the King's palace, the flies in Pharaoh's food, the locusts, the eldest son dead with the whole family in consternation. He also saw Elijah and Elisha cross the Jordan, the chariots of fire, and Elijah's ascension. Daniel was seen in the lion's den with his angel guard, and other Old Testament events were likewise seen.

This boy was also given visions of the miracles of Christ. He saw the temptations of the Lord. The devil in the form of a handsome young man led the Lord to a high mountain and in vision showed Him the Kingdoms of the world. Angels followed Jesus where ever He went. There were visions of Christ walking on the water, healing the sick, and opening the eyes of the blind. This boy and others saw the passion of the Lord Jesus, His resurrection, and His ascension.

At first I wondered at these visions of past events. I then remembered that with God there is no "past," "present," and "future." He is the Great I AM. All things are alike present with Him. Since the Holy Spirit is His Spirit, by visions and His revelations of the Spirit, "past," "present," and "future" may, in God's economy, be made "present" to any individual to whom the Lord chooses to make such revelations.

These revelations of the past to Adullam corroborate the inspiration of the Bible. It was easy for God to take Moses and others by visions through events already past or through future events as an eye witness sees present events and for them to be able to record the past, the present, and the future in the one and only Book that records the end from the beginning and the beginning from the end.

Recording Revelations from God

The Holy Spirit showed us by illustration how some parts of the Bible became divine records of supernatural revelations. When the children were "in the Spirit," describing scenes they were seeing in vision, the Spirit caused one boy, who was also in a trance lost "in the Spirit," to sit down and go through the motions of writing item by item what the others were seeing and describing. Thus anyone should be able to see how easy it was for God to write a Bible. One could record what another saw and described.

If God can now take an ignorant, illiterate beggar boy from a dirty Chinese street, or a half wild little tribes boy from a remote mountain solitude, can fill him with the Holy Spirit, and have him "in the Spirit" escorted by angels see as an eye witness the things beyond the veil—things of the present, things of the past, things to come—has it not always been just as easy for God by visions to reveal everything that is written in the Bible to any vessel of His choosing and have a Barak sit by his side to write just what was seen and revealed, recording word for word any and every prophecy just as it came from the Lord God?

If our boys can be caught into the presence of the Lord and

come back saying, "The Lord said," could not prophets of old even record their own prophecy or visions and say with absolute truth, "Thus saith the Lord?"

How God, with whom past, present, and future is all the same, can reveal past, present, and future events as **present** events, I do not know. The Bible says he can. The Bible says He did. Adullam knows He still does.

If men ever spoke in prophecy as they were moved by the Holy Spirit, if men were ever "in the Spirit on the Lord's Day" and caught up to heaven, if men were ever given visions "in the year King Uzziah died," they can still be moved upon by the Holy Spirit and prophesy. They can still be caught away "in the Spirit" and see the unseen worlds beyond the veil. They can still see visions any number of years after King Uzziah died.

The same God is still on the same throne, reigning over the same world, dealing with the same kind of evil hearts, through the same sort of men, with the same kind of dispositions and passions Elijah had.

Since God does now in this day reveal Himself through prophecy, vision, and revelations—as He is revealing Himself all around the world—he has, therefore, revealed Himself just as the Bible says He did in days of old to the prophets and saints.

In this wicked age, in the midst of this present unbelieving, perverse generation, the Lord can and will prove that what He has written in the Bible is the word of the living God. He can and does move in the midst of a believing people in supernatural ways through gifts of the Holy Spirit, confirming the word with signs following (Mark 16 :15- 20) .

CHAPTER 11

THE HOMELAND

IN VIEW OF WHAT WE HAVE WRITTEN, it is clear enough that the Lord has used every means that is necessary to assure us that in the Bible we have "the sure word of prophecy" to which we should take heed.

It has also been made clear enough that the great purpose of that former word of prophecy and the present day visions and prophecy in our midst is that we may know as a certainty that there is a wonderful homeland just beyond the veil. No "stranger," no "pilgrim" is ever satisfied. The satisfying portion is at the end of the journey.

It may be that as the journey leads over difficult pathways and exhausting mountains the pilgrim becomes so wearied with his heavy burdens that he can scarcely hear the singing of the birds, sense refreshment from the way side flowers, or find any great happiness in the fellowship of his fellow pilgrims. But it will not be so at the end of the way.

The stooped and wearied bodies of life's pilgrims will be renewed by a bath in the fountain of youth when they reach their home in the homeland. "In a moment, in the twinkling of an eye we shall be changed." "This corruptible will put on incorruption." Old age will vanish. There are no old men in heaven, no faltering steps of the aged. No dimmed sight, no deafened hearing, no crippled body encumbers any of the people in the whole of that bright city.

There is a city that never gets dark, nor does it need the sun by day or the moon by night. Its golden streets require no sweeping. Its jewel-bedecked dwellings need no repair. There is a city that has no doctor signs, no diseased and disabled, no sickness or sorrow; a city with no crepe on its golden doors, no funeral processions on its golden streets; a city where melancholy and all mourning is done away; a city where all death has been swallowed up by life and that more abundantly; a city of pure unbounded joy. There is a land of unclouded day where storm clouds never rise. In that happy land there is no bread line or struggle for survival. There is no selfish competition. There is no self-seeking to engender unloving suspicion. No one is anxious as to what he shall eat or what he shall wear. The garments of white will never grow threadbare. The trees with the fruits of life will never be barren.

The water of life will never run dry, and whosoever will may drink.

All the joy and enthusiasm of the most joyful youth is the inheritance of everybody in heaven. But in our most happy days we are still in a vessel of clay. In our highest moments we sense a still greater joy and a happiness almost within the reach of our hands, but ere it can be taken we are dragged away by the weight of the clay. Children frolic and play. They run, and roll, and they leap for joy. They sing and they shout. At times their joy and happiness seem complete. "Of such is the Kingdom of heaven." But the highest exuberant joys and the most ecstatic thrills of bliss of the happiest youth on earth are to be superceded by the greater joy that is "unspeakable" when this body of hindering clay has been replaced by the body that is real.

In the New Jerusalem everybody is "in love." Everybody is in love with everybody else. Being "in love" on earth is as nothing compared with being "in love" in the land of glory. Not a flaw, not an imperfection, not an unlovely trait will detract from being perfectly and altogether "in love" with everybody.

On earth in our encumberance of this depraved tabernacle there is a song in the soul. In its struggle for expression there are times it seems to break out of its restraint for a second, but as quickly the perfect chord is lost. When God made man He put music in his soul. But the discords of the mud have spoiled the harmony. The lost chord will never be found until it is found in heaven when we are clothed upon with the tabernacle that is from above. The finest, the sweetest, the most perfect music on earth is but a seeking for the lost chords and harmonies the redeemed and the angels sing in heaven. The finest instruments of music that have been made on earth, from the days when the sons of Adam began to "handle the harp and pipe" until the present day, are as mere imitations of the trumpets, the harps, and the instruments upon which "the lost chords" are restored in the golden city and upon which all the music of the liberated soul can find its fullest expression.

Much of the music and the rhythm the Father placed in the souls of His children has since been turned by the devil into evil channels for pleasures of the lusts of the perverted flesh. From the wildest barbarians in the mountain fastness to the pleasure intoxicated wild men of the fashionable ball, men dance in musical rhythm to find sensual pleasure that is of the lusts of the flesh. In heaven, to the tune of music that is holy and pure, the redeemed and the angels dance in "joy" that is beyond all earthly or natural "pleasure" in the rhythm to which the stars are swinging and singing in their orbits.

There is a park in the city, an Eden "park of pleasure and fruits." Here, where the unreal has been replaced by the real, in all God's animal and plant creation there is nothing that hurts or destroys in all the holy mount.

On earth we see little and understand less—of the beauties of God's creation. The dirt and the dust of the earth have clouded the windows of our soul. We scarcely see through the glass even darkly. When God has brushed away the encumberances and opened the eyes of the soul, for the first time will we really look upon and appreciate the glories of God's wonderful creation. All this will we do in the Eden over there.

There is a park where the birds of all plumes are ever singing; there is a land where every ear will be tuned to hear their soul-stirring anthems; there is a land where flowers of every hue are ever blooming; there is a land where every eye will be opened to see them in their beauty; there is a land where the fragrance of the rose of Sharon and the lily of the valley mingle with a thousand perfumes that over our world have never blown.

Sometimes we seem to see the light of the city beyond the sky, but our vision is lost in the blur of imperfect sight. Sometimes we seem to hear the enchanting music of a different sphere, but the strain is lost in the discord of sounds that are nearer. Sometimes we seem to sense an upward pull away from all that is enslaving, but the attraction of earth holds our feet like stocks in the fetters that are earthly. Sometimes the soul would fly to "the land that is fairer than day," but it falls back in disappointment because of its broken wings.

He who declares his freedom to walk alone to the city of freedom finds his pathway hopelessly blocked by the things of this world, the flesh, and the devil with no power in himself to overcome.

But there is a way.

CHAPTER 12

THE WAY

THERE IS ONLY ONE WAY. Christ is the way. "No one cometh unto the Father but by me."

Man is not the way, man can never make a way, nor does man ever know the way to the golden city. The city and the way to the city are altogether revelations from above.

Christ, who is the way, is not from below. He is from above. It is "He that descended out of heaven, even the Son of man who is in heaven," who is "the Great God our Savior Jesus Christ."66

Man does not travel toward the happy city of pure delight. He travels away from it. The longer he walks the farther he gets away from this heavenly city. Children belong to the Kingdom of God. They play and frolic at the gates of the city. When they begin to walk alone they always walk away from the city, away from this happy Eden home. The farther they wander and the more they reason — whether they walk alone or follow the crowd—the farther they get from the city, until its light is but dimly seen or lost forever. The only way to reach the city is to turn back. "Except ye turn, and become as little children, ye shall in no wise enter the Kingdom of Heaven!"67 But the farther man walks alone, the older he gets, the richer he becomes; the more he studies with his natural mind, the more he passes turnstiles in his self-conceited course until, at last, the farther turnstiles refuse to move, that should turn him back to a simple faith. He finds no way of returning to a heart like "a little child."

"The world through its wisdom knew not God."68 Man by study will never find God. The man who trusts the workings of his own mind or the minds of other men will never see the city of God.

Man on the merits of his character will never walk the golden streets. What a man is, what a man does, or how a man lives has nothing to do with his salvation. On the basis of how "good" he is, the best man on earth has no more hope of heaven than the worst man on earth. Man who trusts in his own character, his own moral goodness, is only a modern Pharisee with eyes blinded to the truth. The publican, the drunkard, the harlot will enter the city of God, while that "good" man will be cast into outer darkness where is weeping and gnashing of teeth.

"By grace" we are saved, "apart from works." Salvation is something God gives. It is not something man is or is not. Salvation is from above. It is not from below, or from within, or from among men.

That which is born from below is flesh and born by the will of man. Those born from below, no matter how wise or good or bad they may become, must be born again from above. They become the children of God "who were born not of blood, nor of the will of the flesh, nor of the will of man, but of God."69 "Except one be born anew he cannot see the kingdom of God."70 This birth, that every accountable man must have who will ever see God or sing the songs of the redeemed in the city beyond the sky, is a supernatural birth. It is altogether from above. Joining Church, singing hymns, reading or saying prayers, working in or for the church, preaching from the pulpit, or giving all one's body to be burned has nothing whatever to do with the new birth. The new birth is something that God gives by grace regardless of works.

The finest pulpit orator, the most formal churchman, the most protesting protestant has no more hope of heaven than the most reckless sinner, unless he be born again.

How to Find The Way Back Home

The Lord was so anxious to have me return that He made the way simple and plain. I was a sinner living selfishly and not alone for the glory of God. I had turned to my own way. "All have sinned and fallen short of the glory of God."71 "There is none righteous—no not one." "They have all turned aside."72 I was among the number.

Jesus came from heaven to save "sinners," not "righteous people" with good characters. Thus I had my chance. I should have suffered the penalty of my sin, but Christ loved me and died in my stead. He bore my "sins in his body upon the tree."73

Christ died on the Cross the Sinless One instead of the sinner. He "who knew no sin" died in my place on the cross where I should have died. I, the sinning Barabbas, the punishment deserving sinner, was set absolutely and unconditionally free. "He who knew no sin was made sin in our be half."74 God punished Jesus, so He will not punish me. Because He forsook Jesus He will not forsake me. All I had to **be** was to **be** a sinner. All I had to **do** was to **do nothing**.

I simply **believed** that Jesus did it all. "He that believeth hath eternal life."75 "He that believeth hath passed out of death into life."76 To them that believe he gives "the right to become sons of God."77 Having believed that Jesus did what He said He did and having accepted Him as my substitute and as my sin-bearer, He accepted me as His child. He sent His Holy Spirit into my heart, so that I was **born from above**. The Holy Spirit in my heart bore witness, crying, "Abba, Father."78

Before that, I had worked. Now God worked in me to will and do His good will. The things I once loved I now hated, and the things I once hated I now loved. Now the more I try to be good the worse it goes. The more I believe God works in me and for me the better it goes.

The Lord has shown me the light of the city ahead. "I know Him whom I have believed, and I am persuaded that He is able to keep that which I have committed unto Him against that day."[79] I shall surely enter by the gates into the city to share the joys of those who overcome by simple faith because of the blood of the Lamb.

Christ finished salvation. He died for the sins of the whole world. Eternal life is a "gift." "The free gift of God is eternal life."[80] This gift is free. All we have to do is accept it or reject it, take it or ignore it. We must be like one or the other of the thieves on the cross: either believe that Jesus is God and can save a sinner who acknowledges his condition, and spend eternity with Christ in Paradise, or be like the other thief and disbelieve that Jesus is God, and die in our unrepented and unforgiven sins away from God.

Christ saves any and all who are **saved because of their belief**. "Whosoever believeth in Him shall not perish but have eternal life."[81] Those who believe and are thus saved, Christ keeps. They hold not the Rock, but the Rock holds them. They do not hold Christ; Christ holds them. They are **saved** by grace through faith apart from works. They will be **kept** by grace through faith apart from works. "This is the victory that overcometh the world **even our faith**. Who is he that overcometh the world but he that **believeth** that Jesus is the son of God."[82]

The saved by grace and the kept by grace live lives of repentance, do the works of righteousness, and perform religious duties because they are saved already, but not in order to get saved. The work of value they do is because of what God has put **in** them from **above**.

The saved have become "partakers of the divine nature."[83]

"If any man hath not the Spirit of Christ, he is none of his."[84] All of Christ's children have the Holy Spirit in their bodies and hearts and have been born again. "I no longer live but Christ liveth in me."[85] Christ within causes all my works that please him, "For it is God who worketh in you both to will and to work for his good pleasure."[86]

The saved are heavenly citizens who love not the world nor the things of the world. They have as much of the "heaven life" now as they have of the Holy Spirit. The Holy Spirit is the heaven life, the life of God, the eternal life. We have the "earnest," or down payment, of heaven. Through the deeper experiences of the Holy Spirit heaven may become more real than earth, so that the child of God may, at times, almost walk by sight as well as by faith on his pilgrim journey to the city whose builder and maker is God.

Our Adullam message is now complete. This testimony is sent forth, not because of any natural superior knowledge, but because of these things that have happened among us as "God revealed them through the Spirit." [87]

The best we know we cannot write. The best to be known can only be known directly through the revelations of the Holy Spirit to one's own self. More we would write, but more we cannot now write. But what has been written, we have written that you may believe and that "believing you may have life in His name." Or, having life, that you may be encouraged to press onward until you receive more and more of the abundant life, the life through the baptism and fulness of the Holy Spirit, the life the Lord has planned for each of His children, the foretaste and fore-life of the Great City of the King, the city of God where all things are made new.

(Note from GodSounds' editor – corresponding footnotes have not been included in this book. For a full list of the footnotes you may do a quick scan on the internet and find a pdf file of *Visions Beyond the Veil by H.A. Baker* with footnotes included)